Soul Hunger

Sandy Richardson with Susan Wilsie Govier

Soul Hunger

Cover Design by Alpha Advertising
Interior Design by Pine Hill Graphics

Published by Remuda Ranch
Packaged by ACW Press
1200 HWY 231 South #273
Ozark, AL 36360
www.acwpress.com
The views expressed or implied in this work do not necessarily reflect those of ACW Press. Ultimate design, content, and editorial accuracy of this work is the responsibility of the author(s).

Publisher's Cataloging-in-Publication Data
(Provided by Cassidy Cataloguing Services, Inc.)

Richardson, Sandy.

Soul hunger : personal journey / Sandy Richardson with Susan Wilsie Govier. — 1st ed. — Nashville, TN : ACW Press, 2006.

p. ; cm.
(Series on eating disorders)

ISBN-13: 978-1-932124-76-7
ISBN-10: 1-932124-76-4

1. Eating disorders—Psychological aspects. 2. Eating disorders--Treatment. 3. Eating disorders—Religious aspects. 4. Faith. I. Govier, Susan Wilsie. II. Title.

RC552.E18 R53 2006
616.85/26—dc22 0606

Printed in the United States of America.

A Hungry Soul

by
Anne Richardson

I aim for a goal too high to reach
on my own.

A void fills my body; it's all encompassing
Emptiness filling me, and eating at me
from its dark recesses.

No matter how much I eat, or take in, or
give out,
the soul hunger still continues on its
vicious, gnawing path.

Then One comes.
One who feeds and fills.
My mind and soul are satisfied,
And continue to be satisfied with His
incredible love for me.

"I am the bread of life. He who comes to me will never go hungry, and he who believes in me will never be thirsty."

—John 6:35

Table of Contents

Foreword

As I perused the listing of classes our church was offering for the fall quarter, one entitled "Hurts and Healing" intrigued me. I had decided that my husband had some "emotional deficiencies" and that this class might offer him the help he needed. Sandy Richardson was the teacher. I had only a passing acquaintance with Sandy, but I knew a bit of her story.

The first week of class, Sandy began to read a list of words or phrases we use in communicating that indicate "shaming." I was astonished to find not just tears but uncontrollable sobs escaping from my lips. Most shocking was that my weeping was not empathetic, but rather wholly for myself. As my husband gazed at me in bewilderment, Sandy gently hugged me and comforted my inner storm.

This first experience with emotional hurts and healing was revolutionary. Throughout the class, I watched as some people struggled to remain detached, some (like me) cried often and some left, never to return. One thing was clear. We all had "stuff" to work on—emotional baggage. We were looking for survival techniques in a world of conflicting messages and confusing influences.

Throughout the class, Sandy shared openly. Her courage in first facing her illness, then in sharing what she had learned about hurting and healing, became the basis by which we all had more courage to look inside doors we had tried so hard to keep closed.

It has been my great privilege to assist Sandy in this book. By telling her story, Sandy reassures each of us that we are not the only ones to have felt pain, that we don't have to be perfect and, most importantly, that we are never alone.

Susan Wilsie Govier

Preface

I was the fifth patient through the door when Remuda Ranch Center for Anorexia and Bulimia opened in January of 1990. There, in the desert hills of Arizona, my life changed completely and forever. Basking in warm sunshine and excellent care, I took the first tentative steps out of my limited world of fear, distrust and compulsion.

God allowed Ward Keller, founder of Remuda Ranch, to use his experience with his daughter's anorexia to develop a place where thousands have received help and hope. They carry the message of healing literally all over the world.

The staff at Remuda helped me take the first steps along the road to peace and victory. I hope you'll walk that road with me.

Sandy Richardson

Acknowledgments

I owe a deep debt of gratitude to many people for their love and support as I have recovered from bulimia and depression. My husband, Scott, rode the emotional roller coaster with me for 14 years. His love and commitment are what carried me through. We used to just be married—now we're best friends.

To the true friends (and you know who you are) who watched me struggle, stretch and grow, thank you for your steadfast support. You loved the Real Me, even when I wasn't lovable. Kyle, you deserve a crown.

Pastors Donna and Warren Heckman at Lake City Church are a picture of Christ. Thank you for cheering my growth and holding me when I could not stand.

Because of Mom and Pop's courage and willingness to walk through the past and present with me, we now have the relationship I have always hoped for. I love you.

Sue Govier encouraged me years ago to write this book. I could not have written it without her encouragement and guidance. Thanks for your friendship, patience and poetic contribution.

To all the "honorary editors" who made suggestions as I wrote, thank you for having the courage to criticize. Your comments made this a better book. And to my sister, Debbie, thanks for proofreading and listening to me whine when I was discouraged. I love you!

Too Deep for Tears

Thanks to the human heart by which we live,
Thanks to its tenderness, its joys and fears,
To me the meanest flower that blows can give
Thoughts that do too often lie too deep for tears.

—William Wordsworth,
"Ode: Intimations of Immortality
from Recollections Of Early Childhood"

I didn't feel anymore. There was really nothing left to feel, other than the things that weren't allowed. The crosswalk under my feet was becoming slick with the snow that seemed to come too often now, covering all the ugliness of a dead, brown Wisconsin winter in a fresh coat of white. I studied the flake that had settled on my glove and wondered what it would feel like to be covered. What if I just lay down right here and let it bury me? Sighing, I knew it would be no good. I had tried many disguises and none could ever cover the dead brown I had become.

I walked slowly into the airport to board the plane that would take me away. It was all I could do to take the next step. As fearful and apprehensive as one who has decided not to feel can be, I was dimly aware that if I continued living the life I had created for myself, I would not only *feel* dead, but *be* dead.

Somehow that knowledge kept me going. My husband was out of town, my daughters with a friend. Walking alone to the gate, I silently spoke to them. "I'm so sorry, I'm sorry you have been cheated. You thought you had gotten the perfect wife and mommy, but the dead brown started oozing and I couldn't stop it."

What were they feeling? Probably confused and abandoned. I doubted that anything would be changed by this trip, but I had to try; try to stop the decay that had gotten out of control and become my prison. I had responded to an ad suggesting that there was hope for people like me, and I now found myself boarding a plane to give it a try. I considered myself a strong person, but this had beaten me. Let them try to fix me. Pain and fear had dogged me all my life; now it was time to get well or die. One thing was sure: I must change.

To Be Loved, to Be Thin

In the airplane on the way from my home in Wisconsin to Arizona, I had four hours to think about why I was going all the way across the country. All I ever wanted in life was to be thin and to be loved; and for all of my adult life, those two things were mutually exclusive. If I wasn't thin, I wasn't lovable and if I wasn't lovable, it must be because I was fat. If I could just lose enough weight and keep it off, then people would love me—because I would be worthy of their love.

Was being thin and loved really so much to ask? The problem (and I suspected also the reason I was dieting out of control) was that "thin enough" didn't exist. I was so skinny that when I stood with my legs together, my thighs didn't touch. My collarbones stuck out and my ribs showed. I felt some pride because I was thinner than my friends, but I still wanted to lose more. Dieting and craving love was a vicious cycle that had engulfed me.

The longer I thought on that plane, the more depressed I became. What if I couldn't get well? What if there was no hope for me? I devoured the meal I was served, and then threw it up in the cramped airplane bathroom. Shortly after that, the anxiety started to build again, so I ordered wine from the flight attendant and used it to wash down a tranquilizer. Calmer, I stared out the window for the rest of the flight.

Upon landing in Phoenix, I contemplated locking myself in the lavatory until whoever was coming to get me gave up, left me alone and went away. Instead, I found the reserve to walk up the jet bridge. I remembered the brown ooze, and knew that there was no other choice.

Watching me enter the airport concourse, few people would have pegged me as a woman with an eating disorder. At five feet four and one half inches and 115 pounds, I wasn't overweight; yet, by society's standards, I wasn't terribly thin. My hair is my best asset, and it's what people usually remark about. Thick, shiny and bouncy, it fell to my shoulders in a simple pageboy. Even though starvation was causing handfuls to fall out, it still looked good.

My eyes are my other good feature. They're greenish-hazel with a gray band around the iris and gold streaks near the pupil. I have a habit of looking directly into the eyes of others, and now I carefully scanned each face in the waiting area trying to decide who had come to pick me up.

I walked with my shoulders back and head up, a habit left over from my time spent in the military. Usually a direct gaze and purposeful walk helped me feel safer and more in control. Now, as I moved down the corridor, it was an effort to appear confident. A pleasant-looking guy in his forties was holding a card with my name on it, and as I approached him, he smiled and shook my hand. "Hi, I'm Ward," he said. "Let's go get your luggage." I wondered what he was thinking about me as we headed for the baggage area.

The Barrenness of Wrong Choices

A brown and lifeless landscape was all that registered when I first glimpsed the desert southwest. I barely thought about the abrupt change from the snowy weather I had left a few hours ago. Looking back, if it hadn't been so hurtful, I think I would have laughed at the irony. From frozen and infertile to hot and barren—both extremes were a description of my life.

I'd known for a long time that the choices I had been making were wrong. Each morning I'd begin with a vow to myself and to God that today would be different. I would stick to my diet, be a patient and fun mother and a model wife. Above all, there would be no more bingeing and purging, no need to because I would have finally mastered perfection. But by evening I would unfortunately know that, once more, the brown ooze had won and I had lost.

Each day's long list of tasks for the day were again uncompleted. Except for the days I worked at my part-time job with the Air National Guard, the list looked something like this:

Clean bathrooms
Wash windows
Clean out refrigerator
Clean fireplace
Clean litter box

Clean and organize girl's rooms
Grocery shopping
Go to bank, post office, Wal-Mart, craft store
Dinner for family at church
Take girls to ballet

But I couldn't get through even one job without being interrupted by a daughter, the telephone or someone at the door. I would begin one task, then, in another room, find another task I had left and forgotten about. It seemed that nothing ever really got done.

In addition to my lack of productivity, my 1,000-calorie-a-day food plan hadn't lasted past lunch. I hated my weakness and myself. Crawling to my room, I would seek relief from my utter failure, a break that could only be found in sleep.

On a typical day in my world, I would eat a small breakfast consisting of a half cup of Cheerios with skim milk or toast (I never drank juice, it was liquid calories)—then throw it up. After taking the girls to nursery school and kindergarten, I'd go back to bed, too tired and depressed to do anything else. Rising again just in time to shower and pick up the kids, it was then time to deal with lunch. Preparing a healthy meal for my two trusting children came first. They would eat it in front of Sesame Street while I got mine.

My two little girls, Anne and Lauren, were at once my greatest joy and source of insecurity. I wanted very badly to be a wonderful mom to them, but felt I was failing miserably. They were dependent on me for everything when their dad was out of town. While I could provide for them physically, I wasn't able to connect with them emotionally most of the time. My thoughts revolved around myself, my energy drained by the eating disorder.

Anne, who was six, had gentle brown eyes that shone with the wisdom of an old soul. Very intelligent and mature beyond her years, she was serious and possessed the soft beauty of a rosebud. She taught herself to read at age four, and could lose herself in a book or play with her dolls for hours.

Lauren, small for her age at three, was a blue-eyed sprite. Waist-length brown curls flying behind her, she never walked when she could run. "Why?" was her favorite word, and those bright eyes sparkled with fun and mischief. A bundle of energy, she was also quick to climb in my lap for a cuddle and lay her head against my chest while she sucked her thumb.

Anne and Lauren ate their peanut butter and jelly sandwiches, and I began the binge-purge cycle for the day. After eating the half-sandwich (one slice 100 percent whole wheat bread, one slice turkey with mustard, never mayo or cheese), six chips and the apple I had planned, a tightening would begin in my chest and fear would overwhelm me. Miserable, anxious and insatiably hungry, I was consumed by the need to eat. I had to fill my stomach.

Buttons of Pain and Fear

A physical pain I thought of as "Big Button" lodged in the bottom of my stomach, and once the food pressed against it I could begin to feel calm. The binge would begin with a few extra tortilla chips with salsa, then I would think of the ice cream I had bought and have several bowls of that. The strawberry yogurt I got for the kids was next. I only left enough in the carton to prove that I hadn't eaten it all. Then I devoured cookies until I was stuffed to the point of pain.

For a brief moment, I would feel relaxed and numb. But unfortunately Big Button had an evil twin, known as Other

Button, who lived at the top of my stomach. When pushed by all that I had eaten, Other Button triggered a frantic fear. Big Button might be silent, but Other Button was now screaming at me. I had to get all those calories out of my body. Fat was not an option for me. With a stomach so full that my ribs hurt, the Buttons and I would make our way down the hall to the bathroom and begin the ritual.

First, close and lock the master bedroom door. Close and lock the bathroom door. Turn on the faucet and fan to cover my noise. It was then necessary to pull back my hair to keep it clean and drape a towel over my clothes to protect them from the inevitable splatters. Leaning over the toilet, I pushed my finger as far down my throat as it would go.

After throwing up until my stomach was empty and aching, I'd feel relief. Eyes streaming, I would wash my face, brush my teeth and comb my hair. Next the toilet, floor, and walls needed to be scrupulously cleaned to remove any evidence. Carefully wiping up with the spray bottle of disinfectant and paper towels kept under the sink for that purpose, I would be glad that I had papered the walls with easy-to-clean vinyl wallpaper. Last, I drank a huge glass of cold water so my stomach wouldn't feel so empty.

Although my stomach cramped and my throat stung, I felt better. The food was gone and so was the fear of getting fat. I had a rush of energy, and tried to ignore the guilt and remorse. How could I have done it again? Every single day I prayed that today I could stop. God knew I failed, seeing me fall short of perfection every time. In Jeremiah 23:24, God's Word tells us that He is everywhere: " 'Can anyone hide in secret places so that I cannot see him?' declares the LORD. 'Do I not fill heaven and earth?' declares the LORD."

My perfect manicure was marred and my knuckles were scraped from my forced vomiting. I tried very hard not to look at my hands since they reminded me of my sin. I couldn't hide my bulimia from God, but if I was very careful I could hide it from others. No one knew, or even suspected, and I had to keep it that way.

The remainder of my day was busy with children, housekeeping and errands. We lived in a typical vinyl-sided, split-level ranch home. A large screened porch on the back looked over lots of trees. I loved our house, and took pride in keeping it neat and decorating it with flea market finds and handmade accessories. I painted the fireplace brick dark red, and made complementary blue and red curtains for the living room and dining room. The girls each had homemade matching curtains and bedspreads, and the master bedroom was an oasis of soft yellow, pinks and greens. At the time, I defined "clean and pretty" as "perfect"—and I could never meet my own standards.

By late afternoon, exhausted and starving, I would get a snack for the girls and allow myself "a couple" of cookies or crackers. Actually I would nibble until the bag was empty, and then become furious with myself.

Repeated Ritual

Back in the bathroom, it was time to go through the purging ritual all over again. Once done, I would emerge feeling more powerful and back in control. I then felt sure I could eat a small dinner and spend the evening checking all the items off my chore list, which had been barely touched through this day on the battlefield.

After dinner, which was invariably low-fat, meatless and high fiber, I'd sneak off to the bathroom to purge yet again. I was always very careful not to let my husband know what I was doing. My own self-hatred level was high enough. I imagined how horrified and disgusted he would be if he knew. When he was home, I restricted what I ate to avoid having to purge. Sometimes the urge to binge would be too great, and I would eat a small dinner, then all of the leftovers as I cleaned up after the meal. Terrified of gaining weight, I'd claim that I had an errand to run and get in the car to go purge in a gas station restroom. On occasion, I'd go for a walk and throw up in the woods or a trashcan in an alley.

In bed at night, I would tell myself that this was the last day of such behavior and pray for strength to stop bingeing and purging. Starting tomorrow, my life would be different. I would begin to lose weight, work out more. Soon I'd have thin thighs, long nails, perfect hair and a flat stomach.

I claimed to be devoted to my Lord and my family, but my top priorities were how I looked and what other people thought of me. I never went out in public without being neatly dressed, with every hair in place and makeup perfect. I wanted to appear to be an all-American Christian woman—modestly but fashionably clothed, thin, witty and well educated. If I could maintain that veneer, then no one would ever guess what I had once been.

In my past I dressed provocatively to attract men's attention. I loved to party and I had a foul mouth. "Bad" language was not tolerated in my family while I was growing up, but I learned to swear really well while in the military. Almost all of my coworkers had a very colorful vocabulary, and before long I picked it up. After I married and gave my life to Christ, I worked hard at cleaning up my act and my image. If I couldn't make myself good on the inside, I could alter my outward appearance so that I would look blameless.

Out of the Closet

Once, right after Scott and I married in 1981, he noticed that I disappeared after supper and returned looking pale. I had just read a letter to Ann Landers in the newspaper, and for the first time discovered that I hadn't invented my problem. Not only that, it had a name. I was bulimic. I confessed to Scott that I was making myself throw up and that I was afraid. He was shocked, but true to his practical character, he advised me to "just stop doing it."

I was hurt that Scott didn't offer sympathy or suggestions. I didn't understand at the time that his answer didn't reflect a lack of compassion, but his personality. He is a pilot, and certain characteristics are common to most people in his profession. They're intelligent and unemotional. Perfectionists, they have high standards for themselves and others. They're compulsive about being in control, and tackle problems head-on, confident in their ability to overcome. Their qualities make them safe, effective pilots. Scott didn't understand that by confessing my fear and pain to him, I had already acknowledged that I needed help. I didn't understand that I was already so deeply entrenched in my behavior that I would need professional help to stop. Purging was the only way I knew to feel in control.

There were only two other times in the next nine years of our marriage that Scott found out that I was purging. Once I had made a batch of homemade scones that my family loved. We made a pot of tea, and I ate four scones at one sitting. I went to the bathroom, locked the door and threw them back up. When I came out, Scott was sitting on our bed, looking at me with a mixture of anger and bewilderment.

"Are you still making yourself vomit?" he asked.

"Um, no," I lied, "I just had to use the toilet." The truth was that by then it was far too late for me. I could no longer control my eating disorder. It controlled me.

"Are you lying to me?" asked Scott.

"No, no, really, I'm not doing that any more," I said, looking at my feet. I couldn't meet his eyes.

I had always hated my body. As a short, skinny child, I was teased that if I turned sideways and stuck out my tongue, I'd look like a zipper. I was such a stick that I could take a small footstool, put the legs around my upper body, and the stool would slide right down to the floor.

When I reached puberty, I began to grow taller and put on weight. In my own eyes, I was bigger and heavier than all of my friends. Insecurity in my appearance began to haunt me. Looking back, I can see from photos that I was actually of average height and weight, but somehow in my own mind I felt big and clumsy. Self-hatred led to depression, and I confided to my mother that I thought I was overweight. She validated my concern by taking me to our family doctor. The 1,000 calorie-a-day diet he prescribed for me that day at the age of 14 marked the beginning of a cycle of dieting and overeating that would continue for the next 20 years.

Food had always made me feel better. When I was sad or lonely or angry, eating lulled me into a relaxed state in which things didn't seem so bad or scary. Two cookies would stop hunger pangs, but six gave me a sense of well-being when I was anxious or sad. After school, potato chips dipped in blue cheese dressing made the world look better if I had failed a math test or messed up at band practice. Food became my solace after fights with my parents or sister.

In a very real sense, food became my best friend and worst enemy. I wanted food, looked forward to eating it, even dreamed about it—and regretted every bite I ate. I loved food and feared becoming fat. This dysfunctional relationship with food so consumed my life that it seemed there was no way out.

When, after many battles, I finally lost weight, I would become terrified that I would gain it back again. Every day became a battle of wills. Bingeing and purging became the best way I had found to satisfy my desire for food without paying the price. It seemed that if I could control my weight while still appeasing the emotional food monster constantly calling to me, I could have my cake and eat it too.

A Call to Be Healed

It was through this chaos, created over the years of fear and pain, that I finally heard my heavenly Father calling out to me. It had been a day like any other, of chasing kids and attempting to clean my house. In a state of lethargy, I absently turned the pages of a magazine as I ate the sandwich I knew would be the beginning of the cycle for the day. I was reading a Christian magazine in an attempt to feel encouraged, but instead the articles seemed to point out my weakness and sin. The pantry, only a few steps away, was filled with the foods that made me feel better. I knew the relief would be only temporary. The salsa and sharp chips would be painful coming back up.

My eyes suddenly fell upon a full-page ad in the magazine and I stopped chewing. The ad said, "We can help women suffering from anorexia and bulimia." I was stunned. I knew that what I was doing had a name, but I had no idea there were enough women like me to warrant a hospital. "Our Christ-centered approach allows each guest to build the confidence to deal with the problems and stresses of everyday life without starving, bingeing or purging," the ad said. A Christian treatment center? A chance to go away and stop my sickening behavior? I felt a brief flicker of hope. What would it be like to eat and not hate myself?

With heart pounding, I dialed the number in the ad. The woman who answered the phone asked me hard-hitting, direct questions. How often did I eat so much that I was angry with myself? What did I eat at each meal? Did I weigh myself daily? How many times a day did I purge? I was amazed! She knew exactly what I was doing. I wondered if she could see inside my bathroom and me. It was hard to hear her say that bulimia was dangerous. The pressure I was putting on my heart, stomach and esophagus could be fatal.

The counselor also said that I didn't have to spend the rest of my life obsessed with food and my body. She offered me hope. Could it be possible for me to escape the endless cycle of thinking about food, denying myself food and gorging on food? The shameful behavior I hid in the bathroom was so much a part of my life, I couldn't imagine I had any other choice.

That night when Scott came home, I confessed to him that I had been anorexic and bulimic for the entire nine years of our marriage. Understandably, he was shocked and angry. Telling him I had found a hospital to treat me didn't exactly calm him. He had watched me grab at many straws over the years in an attempt to feel better. I had tried diets, hormone therapy, vitamins and psychological therapy. Not surprisingly he saw this as another desperate attempt—and a very expensive one.

I assured him that our insurance would pay for almost all of it, but that still left many obstacles if I was going to leave home for a few months. He reminded me that someone would have to stay with the girls while he traveled. I would need to take a leave of absence from my job, and I'd have to call my parents and tell them what was going on. I also had to consider what to tell my friends. I couldn't just disappear for a long time and leave Scott holding the bag when they started to ask questions.

The first and most difficult task was to tell my parents. I wanted so badly for them to think that I was a good person after my rebellious behavior as a child and teenager and my rocky times in college. I didn't know if they'd ever heard of bulimia, and I wasn't looking forward to introducing them to it. My fears were unfounded. They both expressed sincere concern and love for me, saying they wanted to do whatever they could to help me get well. They also solved part of my other big concern, child-care. Offering to be with the girls either at my house or at theirs helped Scott and me immensely. Scott's parents also graciously offered help with the children and showed concern for my well-being.

I called my commander at the Air National Guard and told him I had some problems related to my family that needed my attention. After I told him I was the only one in the family who had the means to go all the way to Arizona to settle the issue, he gave me the time off and sent his good wishes with me.

Lamentable Lies

Combined with my relief to be dealing with my disease, I was also beginning to feel like a real rat. I not only lied to my boss, but also to my friends. I told them that I had severe PMS and was going to a special clinic in the southwest that treated such problems. All but one of them bought it. Kathie is a nurse, and she knew that there weren't any "PMS clinics." She called me back after we talked and asked me what was really going on. When I admitted I had an eating disorder, she told me she had spent some time working in an eating disorders program and reassured me that I could get well. That calm acceptance helped give me the courage to write to my other friends while I was in treatment and tell them the truth.

The night before I left, Scott was on a trip. I took Anne and Lauren to Pizza Hut for dinner. Pizza was as close to fast food as we usually got. They happily ate their "little pizzas" and I ate a large serving of pasta and several slices of garlic bread. During the meal, I talked to them about my going away. I told them that I was sick and had to go to a special hospital. They were confused because I didn't really look sick. Both were concerned that I might die. Telling them that people with my sickness didn't usually die, I prayed I was right. I knew eating disorders are often fatal, but I couldn't tell my young daughters they might never see their mother again.

After eating, we went to my best friend's house where the girls would stay until my parents could get there to pick them up. She was gone for a few minutes after I arrived, so I put the kids in front of the TV and sneaked off to the bathroom to quickly get rid of my dinner. I was disgusted with myself and crying by the time Kyle got home. She assumed it was because I was leaving my children, but really I was just revolted by my lack of self-control.

It was hard to realize that I wouldn't see my babies again for a long time. Lauren cried and, after hugging me, sucked her thumb and watched me with big eyes. Anne said good-bye like a little adult and told me to hurry and get better so I could come home. Driving home, I felt wretched. Why on earth couldn't I be normal like everyone else I knew?

Ten days after the initial phone call to the treatment center, I watched the snow-covered ground fall away beneath the airplane. I had no idea what anyone at the clinic could do to help me, but I had to try. I had no more illusions. I would not go home and pick up the same painful, paralyzing routine.

I had also decided that as long as I was paying for treatment, I might as well take along all of my other problems. I pictured my pain and confusion as a large, smelly canvas bag leaking brown ooze. I carried it with me everywhere. That ooze represented many things. Feelings of inferiority, that I was never good enough. The feeling that I could never measure up or be loved. I was dirty because of my past, helpless to change my present and hopeless about my future.

I had no idea at that time that my eating disorder and my inner turmoil were closely related. All my life I had been miserable, always running from something. I didn't know why, and I couldn't explain my feelings. They were just an integral part of me.

During the drive into the Arizona desert, I couldn't begin to imagine the answers that were locked up inside my heart. I felt numb. Pushed down, buried and protected by all the years of pretending, my pain was too deep for tears.

The First Steps

A journey of a thousand miles must begin with a single step.

—Lao-Tzu, c. 604-531 B.C.

The drive to the treatment center was safe. Polite conversation, acceptable distance—these were skills I had mastered. The driver hadn't asked, "So why are you a bulimic?" and I hadn't asked, "So what do you think of a woman who throws up after every meal?" I looked at my fingernails, scrutinizing them for dirt or flaws. Not too bad, I decided. Certainly this guy would not notice any failings, for he was dressed in jeans, western boots and a T-shirt that looked as though it had seen better days. Besides, why should I care what he thought? I didn't even know him. But I did care. What people thought of me mattered very much.

I asked my driver what he did at the treatment center, and he told me that he was just the guy who carried suitcases and drove the van. The more we talked, the harder that was for me to believe. He seemed much too knowledgeable about the treatment center to be only a driver. I tried again. "Are you a therapist or a doctor?" Finally he laughed and told me that he was the owner of the center. That really surprised me.

Further questioning revealed that this treatment center was brand-new and unique. Ward explained that Remuda Ranch actually was a ranch, not a typical hospital. He and his wife had turned their own home into a treatment center, hired professionals to develop and run a program and achieved accreditation as a mental health care facility. They decided to open it for women with eating disorders after struggling to find professional Christian treatment for their daughter who suffered from anorexia at the age of 10.

When Ward informed me that I would be the fifth patient to be admitted, I thought, "What have I gotten myself into? A brand-new center that's really a ranch?" It was nice to know that I wouldn't be trapped in a sterile hospital environment, but now I wondered about the experience level of the staff. What if they didn't know what they were doing?

Finally I remembered my favorite lines spoken by Scarlett O'Hara in the movie "Gone With The Wind": "I won't think about that today. If I do, it will drive me crazy. I'll think about that tomorrow." And I let denial comfort me for the rest of the ride.

Arriving at the treatment center, I felt relieved to have taken the first big step—and afraid of what was to come. Now that I was here, it was clear that something was supposed to happen, but I had no idea what. A white fence bordered the long driveway to the main building. There were horses grazing in a pasture and a scattering of adobe buildings. I was delivered to the largest one.

I felt out of place in my dress and nice shoes. The dress I was wearing was a part of my carefully constructed front. It was supposed to say that I was intelligent, educated and normal—a lot to expect from a simple, long-sleeved dress. I wouldn't wear the nylons and uncomfortable clothes for long. It was a relief to see that everyone, from the man who met me at the airport to the nurses and other patients, was dressed in jeans and western boots or sneakers. I was very depressed and knew that just taking a shower and blow-drying my hair every day would be a challenge, so not having to "dress up" was welcome news.

I was left alone to change clothes and immediately went to the French doors in my room. Through the panes of glass I could see a patio and emerald lawns with cactus gardens. I was surprised that grass could be so green in such a hot place. In the distance a wide, dry riverbed lined with trees meandered off into the horizon. There were mountains, clouds and a very blue sky. It didn't look like a bad place to be and I wondered if it would be safe to relax a little. But self-preservation won over the hospitable atmosphere. I decided to stay on my guard a little longer.

My Life from A to Z

Now in jeans and sneakers, I went to the front office to be checked in. The first order of business turned out to be a long interview. The mental health technician who conducted it asked for the story of my life. I was asked everything from simple questions such as what I ate for breakfast to difficult, personal questions.

I had to describe in detail every single aspect of my life. What were my relationships like with my mother and father? My first thought was "Ha! Have you got a few hours?" Instead, I answered that I wasn't extremely close to my parents, but I got along better with my mother than I did with my stepfather. I was intimidated by him and a little afraid of him. I knew that my mom loved me, but wasn't so surc about my step dad. Mom and I talked several times a month, but our conversations rarely went further than surface things. We both seemed to recoil from anything emotional. I believed that both my parents were profoundly disappointed with me. I felt that in their eyes the only positive and productive thing I had ever done was marry a good man and have children.

Had I ever taken illegal drugs, fought with my siblings or been arrested? "Yes, Yes and Yes," I wanted to say and leave it at that. The details were painful to me. However, I politely answered that my siblings and I fought constantly as children, sometimes physically hurting each other. I had a stepbrother who beat me up and locked me in closets. My sister and I spent almost our entire childhood disliking each other. When we were teenagers, it was my special delight to torment her. She seemed beautiful and perfect and everything I wanted to be but couldn't.

As for drugs, I tried marijuana in college, but didn't tell the counselor how much I had liked it or that I lied about my drug use to get into the military. My criminal past was simpler to explain. Just the year before I had been arrested at a pro-life rally for trespassing when I refused to leave the crowd of people blocking the door to an abortion clinic. I was proud of myself for taking a stand against abortion, and was surprised that I hadn't been arrested before. Some of my college behavior had gone beyond outrageous to illegal. The woman interviewing me raised her eyebrows when I told her about the arrest but made no comment.

How did I feel before, during and after a binge and purge? "Hungry, stuffed, guilty" seemed to be an appropriate answer, but I tried to explain the gnawing hunger that food only temporarily satisfied. My whole body felt empty before a binge, not just my stomach. I ached to be filled from my feet to the top of my head. During a binge I was frantic—afraid of being caught, ashamed of what I was doing and anxious to be through. Once finished I had momentary peace, lulled into comfort because I no longer felt empty. It never lasted long enough, though.

Especially humiliating was trying to describe the physical and mental sensations I experienced while I purged. Purging hurts. It's not like throwing up when I had the flu. Stomach acid that was freshly produced to help digest the food came up too, and it stung and burned my throat and mouth. A raw, acidic sensation filled my sinus cavities and nostrils and made it hard to breathe. Most of all, I was disgusted by my behavior as I imagined myself hunched over the toilet with my hand stuck down my throat. The interviewer just nodded and took notes.

How had I done in school? "I hated school and I would never want to revisit high school or college," I replied. School was merely one more area in my life where I could not measure up. In high school I longed to be popular and a cheerleader. I envied the cheerleader's willowy figures, long straight hair and air of self-confidence. My grades were good except for math, but because I couldn't get more than a "C" in that subject, I felt like an idiot. Marching band was the only place I felt like part of a group, but I couldn't sight-read music and so I felt like a failure there, too.

College was at once a relief and a nightmare. I had dreamed of being on my own, and I was. I worked full-time and attended classes, desperate to get a degree that would allow me to support myself when I graduated. I drank heavily and dated frequently to dull my feelings of incompetence and self-hatred. Many hangovers and destructive relationships later, I was still insecure and had more reasons to dislike myself. I studied as little as I could and still pass my classes. I graduated with a pathetic grade-point average and a profound sense of gratitude that I was finished with school. It wasn't "summa cum laude"; it was more like "Thank You, Laude."

Did I feel close to my children, and how would I describe my husband? I felt like a total failure as both wife and mother, but all I said was, "We get along fine." Telling her about Scott, I said that he was wonderful and I meant it. I felt lucky to have such a great and supportive husband, but I also felt sorry for him. He was stuck with a sick and incompetent wife. My children were clean, reasonably well behaved and seemed all right emotionally, but I knew that I wasn't a very good mother. It bothered me that I felt relieved when they were at school or asleep. They deserved someone who could get the housework done and still have time to play with them on the floor. A good mommy would bake cookies with them and not be bothered by the mess.

The questions all targeted my insecurity, and as sarcasm bubbled up within me I forced myself to answer politely and automatically, feeling detached from the process. I picked at my cuticle, working at its imperfection, feeling no pain as I tore a hangnail from its bed. As the questions mounted, I began to feel as though the brown ooze was creeping out of me to engulf me in its nasty morass.

Had I ever been raped or sexually abused? As my mouth formed the word No, I began to feel hot and sweaty. I stopped picking my nail. In my memory I dimly saw my face in a mirror, pale, frightened and ugly. I was 17 again, in the bathroom of the house where I grew up. There was a burning and stinging between my legs. I felt the terror and shame of having been raped an hour earlier on the floor in the back room of a pet store where I worked. Blinking, I said, "Wait, yes. I have been raped." How could I have forgotten something that horrible and significant? I was embarrassed, and wondered if the woman interviewing me thought I was lying. Where had that memory been? What if there were more hiding in some deep wrinkle of my brain?

After completing the interview, checking my suitcase and confiscating my tranquilizers and razor, I was left alone in my room. I had packed for two weeks, figuring that would be plenty of time for the doctors to make me stop throwing up and tell me what I was doing to make my life and myself so miserable. My suitcase was full of drab clothes. I brought old T-shirts and jeans, nothing pretty and no accessories. It seemed that somewhere in my mind I had decided that since I felt like pond scum, I ought to dress the part. By presenting myself there, I was admitting that I was deeply flawed, and I was afraid that the others would think me pathetic if I tried to look too classy.

Settling In

My room was large, with two single beds made of massive pine logs, a couch and two desks. French doors led to a small patio with large chairs. As I took all this in, I unpacked and put the pictures of my girls on the desk next to my bed. A sign was propped up on the pillow that said, "Welcome Sandy! We're glad you're here." Four women, whom I assumed were the other patients, had signed it. I had been told that they were all in a therapy group. I would meet them at dinner.

Dinner. I was glad I had arrived after lunch. That was one less meal to deal with. I wanted to curl up on the bed and try to nap for a while. Stop the thinking, remembering and confusion the interview had brought, and prepare mentally for the meal I was about to face. But there was not enough time and the attendant had made it clear that I was expected. She said that everyone was looking forward to meeting me. Right. They were only being nice because I was paying to be there. Smiling, I desperately hoped I could keep the ooze from showing.

When dinnertime came, I walked across the hall to the dining room, struck by how much this place looked like someone's house instead of a hospital. The hall was wide, and hung with a portrait of a family in a western setting. There was a funny little table, made of a piece of wood on top of a pair of legs dressed in blue jeans and cowboy boots. A small sign on it read, "Here lies Clyde who wouldn't be neat. He came in the house without wiping his feet." That didn't seem like something you would find in a hospital.

The dining room was large and bright, with sliding doors leading to a patio. Along one wall was a nurse's station. A long table was set with cloth place mats and napkins. Blue cushions were on the chairs. The kitchen was right there, too, separated from the dining room by a tiled counter lined with tall stools.

As we sat down, I was faced with an overwhelming rush of anxiety. The other women at the table with me were thin. I was thin, but compared to them I felt like an elephant. I was told that these women were seriously anorexic, but to me they looked perfect. They were introduced, and each one told me a little about herself.

Patty, who was my roommate, was a pastor's wife with four children, from another southwestern state. Tall and graceful, she had been anorexic since her teens and had been through treatment before. She had beautiful hazel eyes and an easy smile, and didn't look sick to me. Ruth, in her 40s, was the oldest patient there and the most severely underweight. She lived with her husband and son a short distance from the center. Having been treated before, she said that she really wanted to get over her anorexia which she had developed as a child.

Sarah was a bundle of nervous energy. She spoke with a real Texas twang, and gestured with her hands as she talked. A bulimic, she was in her umpteenth hospital stay. Her teeth bore the discolored signs of someone who purged a lot. Ginny seemed very gentle. Her large brown eyes were sad as she told me about the little girl she had to leave at home when she came here. Though in her 20s, Ginny had already survived a couple of heart attacks brought on by excessive purging. All of the women were so nice that I decided to forgive them for being thinner than I.

My second dilemma was on the plate in front of me. Stir-fried vegetables and beef with white rice. What was a vegetarian, health food fanatic to do? I ate the vegetables and pushed the rest of it around with my fork, under the watchful eye of the staff member who had interviewed me.

New Men in My Life

During the meal, two men walked through the dining room at different times. Don was introduced as my primary therapist. He wasn't tall, but he had presence. With a smile on his face, he had a good word for each of the patients. As he shook my hand and looked at me with intense eyes, I could tell already I was going to have a hard time fooling him.

The second man to enter the dining room was a mental health technician. The other patients laughed at a poster he had put up in the kitchen. It had a cartoon of a pile of peas on the planet Earth, along with a big circle of cheese and two goofy-looking guys. Under the drawing was printed, "Peas on earth, gouda wheel two men." I began to feel that I had made a serious mistake. In the first place, this wasn't a joke. In the second place, no one had said anything about men being here. The man who picked me up in Phoenix didn't count. He wasn't involved in the treatment process.

I didn't like men, and didn't trust them. All my life had been spent trying to please men, but failing. They sat in constant judgment of my every motive and action. In no way did I want them involved in my life as a patient. One of the male counselors told me later that if looks could kill he would have been toast. It became my plan to completely ignore them for as long as it took them to get the message. Fortunately, they had thick skin and were prepared for me. It wasn't long before they both became impossible to ignore.

As my therapist, Don intended to know everything about me. A Texan, he had the accent to prove it. I recognized his dry sense of humor immediately and knew that I would be most comfortable joking with him. I had discovered years before that looking people directly in the eye usually made them uncomfortable and they would look away. During our first session, I tried it with Don, but to no avail. He had kind eyes, but the more I revealed about myself, the harder it became to look at him. As my deepest, darkest secrets spilled out, I was certain he would become disgusted with me. However, the most dramatic reaction I ever got was a raised eyebrow and a casual "So?"

Don approached me first with unconditional love and acceptance, and only later with questions. And he smiled a lot, both with his mouth and his eyes. One day I toyed with the idea of telling him that I had been an ax murderer, just to see what he'd say. Knowing him, he probably would have said, "I'm sure Jesus has forgiven much worse things." I needed that calm acceptance so much at that time in my life. I had spent years trying to hide and forget my past and to appear perfect to others. Now I was being encouraged to lay it all bare; and instead of being rejected and judged, as I feared, I found acceptance and a purpose for reliving my past.

As I progressed in treatment, Don helped me make connections between things that happened to me as a child and my adult behavior and feelings. Helping me see the logical association of early trauma with choices I made as an adult, he told me that I wasn't "bad," I had just made poor choices. Because of his unconditional acceptance, I felt comfortable revealing more of myself to him. Don was easy to respect and take seriously because he told me the truth—gently, but without sugarcoating it. My patient-therapist relationship with him paved the way for trusting other men in my life, especially my husband.

Even with excellent professional care, looking back at my journal from the first week of treatment I can see that it records my feelings of confusion, depression and fear. It was a busy week. Besides sessions with Don, I had to take mental health assessment tests, go to the local hospital for blood work and x-rays, be thoroughly examined by the physician at the center and see a psychiatrist for an evaluation. Plus, between all of the tests, I was introduced to various therapy groups. I wondered if I was ever going to get down to the business of getting well. I was homesick and constantly anxious because I couldn't binge or purge. How I longed to throw up! Yet through all my thoughts was a sense of awe at the beauty of the high desert, and a sense of security at the homelike atmosphere of the center.

A Place to Breathe Again

Outside, the mountains rose in the distance. The gently sloped landscaping of the grounds provided pathways and resting places for meditation and contemplation. Scattered adobe buildings and fenced corrals full of horses gave me the impression of a snug but purposeful place. The air was dry and pungent with the scent of mesquite. I loved sitting outside with the sun beating down on me, feeling as though I had been dropped into a picture postcard. Although I didn't realize it in those first frightening days, something inside me seemed to know even then that this was a place where it might be possible to breathe again. Maybe I could grow my nails long and perfect.

The rustic log interior of the main lodge was filled with details that radiated comfort and relaxation. From the tongue-and-groove knotty pine-paneled walls and rough-hewn log furnishings to the baby grand piano, loaded down with well-used sheet music, the overall sense was one of a very different place, set aside a little bit from the hurried pace of the outside world. Pine couches with big comfy cushions were lined up in front of the TV. Every night before dinner, we patients would pile onto a couch and watch the news or a game show after a busy, emotional day.

I would like to say that I enjoyed those first days, but honestly I was so used to filling up every moment of my day with work that it was hard to relax. With our notebooks, Bibles, journals and stuffed animals strewn all over the great room, it looked like a bunch of kids lived there. We all had assigned chores before we ate, and I felt a little like a kid again as I folded napkins and helped set the table.

From "Fine" to Frank

The other patients were very friendly and encouraging. The staff was both kind and firm. Nurses, therapists and mental health techs focused all day, every day, on our feelings. While I could always tell people what I *thought*, talking about what I felt was more of a challenge. After about the fifth time Don asked me how I felt and I said I felt "fine," he told me that "fine" stands for "Fouled-up, Insecure, Neurotic and Emotional."

"Fine" was the cloak I wrapped myself in so that no one could see my bruises. Hiding my emotions behind the protection of "fine" had become second nature. I had to learn a new vocabulary to express my emotions. With prompting, I began to realize that angry, irritated, calm, anxious, scared, happy, peaceful, sad and many other words were useful in telling someone how I felt.

Patty, Ruth, Sarah and Ginny guided me through those first bewildering days and made me feel at home as much as possible. After only a week, I felt that I knew them better than some of the people I had known all of my life. I found comfort in my newly emerging, dysfunctional family of other lonely people who I would come to recognize were a lot like me. Listening to others tell about their unusual eating behaviors, laxative abuse and strained relationships helped me to feel strangely at home. No one I knew "back home" was this honest about themselves and their lives.

A new picture of "normal" was beginning to emerge. My idea of normal was to be happy, energetic, productive and even tempered—all of the time. I was discovering that while addictions are certainly not normal, we were not abnormal because we had afflictions that had led to addictions. Even the staff was reassuringly vulnerable about themselves and their lives. They told us that everyone has pain and trials in their lives. Healthy people face the pain and work through it. Unhealthy people lie about it, cover it up and resort to addictive behavior to dull it or deny that pain exists for them. It was a new and revolutionary concept for me. All of the people I had compared myself to and considered perfect *weren't*.

My friends, for instance. Talented, pretty, cheerful, they seemed to have perfect lives. And the people at church—they did so much for God and for other people, and I never heard them talk about any personal troubles. Certainly, I knew people who had marriage problems or serious illnesses, but comparing my life to theirs left me feeling guilty because they were so noble and I was such a mess. But now I was discovering that everyone is human, and that if I asked the right questions or looked closely enough I would see that they had struggles of their own. The difference between mental illness and health was the ability to face problems head-on rather than run from them. Now the people I admire the most aren't the ones who have no problems, but the ones who bear them the most gracefully.

One thing I really resented about the program was the loss of personal choices. I was followed to the bathroom, couldn't go outside alone and was told where to go and what to do every minute of the day. It was all I could do not to get really rude and in-your-face toward the patient, quiet followers who now knew all my bodily functions and habits. The treatment program was designed so that freedom and privileges were assigned as progress was gained. They were applying the psychology that temporarily giving up control was essential to getting well.

The Days of My Life

My days were filled with community meetings, chapel, therapy sessions, group discussion, and art therapy, horse grooming and riding. It was exhausting. Even free time was filled with required reading, journaling and therapy assignments.

Every day began with a meeting of the patients before breakfast. We discussed details of living together, such as whose turn it was to set the table and rules for the laundry room. It was the staff's chance to make announcements to us as a group, and our chance to ask questions or voice concerns. (Can we have longer telephone privileges? Why can I only have one cup of coffee with meals? Do we get to go shopping?)

After breakfast was chapel. It was intimate, with the patients and a staff member sitting on couches in a circle. We started with prayer, sang a few choruses and then the staff member "of the day" would give a short meditation to encourage us as we began another day of mining our souls. Bonnie, who was my admissions advisor, always ended with "Work hard today, girls!" We needed to hear that, because for most of us our prayer was "Help me to have a good day today, Lord." For me, "good" meant no scary feelings. But Bonnie knew that without facing the scary stuff, we couldn't progress in recovery. Chapel ended with more prayer for potential patients who had called and were thinking about coming.

"Didactic" Group was next on the day's schedule. Didactic is a fancy word for teaching, and in this group I was introduced to concepts of mental health that were new to me. From the basics of personality to family dynamics, I began to gather information that gave me a glimmer of how to put my life back together. I was learning the "whys" of eating-disordered behavior, from its roots to its addictive components. Finding all this fascinating in an intellectual sense and personally enlightening, I drank it in.

Traveling from the brain to the heart, "Process" Group therapy came next. After a walk down the hill to a small building and a cozy room with a piano and fireplace, we got down to business. In this group we talked about ourselves. This was the place to discuss what hurt. All of those unidentified feelings I had been running from for so long were rediscovered here.

The other patients were very open in Process Group. They talked about experiences from their childhood and how these experiences tied in to their eating disorder. As different ones described scenes from their lives with parents, husbands and children, I felt more normal. I wasn't the only one to have binged and purged, lied and covered up. Their insight into their "issues" (the problems or trauma that had prompted the eating disorder) and illness impressed me. Ginny's mother had been a model, and extremely beautiful and talented. That had been very hard to live up to. Sarah had always wanted to please her father, but never felt she could. Ruth had become the mother and housekeeper for her family at a very young age.

The sexual abuse, perfectionism, abandonment and neglect they described were the reason they were there. Their eating disorders had been born when they discovered that controlling their weight and the amount of food they ate gave them another focus. When every minute of the day is spent thinking about food and the size and shape of your body, there's no time or energy left for emotional pain.

I had no insight into my own life whatsoever. Listening to them, I really wanted someone to tell me what my issues were, what I needed to understand and work on. My desire was to get it out, get over it and go home. I had always been strong willed, striving to make everything turn out the way I thought it was supposed to. It seemed obvious to me that the problems that had created my eating disorder simply needed to be identified, categorized and resolved. In the same way I tied my kid's shoes and buttoned their clothes out of impatience rather than teaching them to do it, I wanted someone to tell me what my problem was so I could get on with solving it. Luckily, God's way is much more gentle. I now know I could not have survived having all of my own deep hurts revealed to me at once.

After Process Group, it was back up the hill for lunch at the main lodge, when we got to practice eating while feeling strong emotions. Many days I sat and stared at my food, knowing I was so anxious that after I ate I was going to want to purge. On the other hand, not eating presented another problem: having to drink a chalky-tasting liquid nutritional supplement. After a few rounds of that, eating became the more attractive alternative. Once or twice another patient or a nurse sat with me and held my hand, telling me that I'd make it through without throwing up. After a while it got easier, but I often dreaded lunch.

Hooked on Horses

In the afternoon, we went to what I considered the strangest therapy group of all. It was simply called "Equine." We walked to the stables and were met by Rosie, the equine therapist. In her Wranglers and cowboy hat, Rosie was the first real "cowperson" I had ever met. She was tall, with sun-weathered skin and compassionate, deep-blue eyes. An expert equestrian, she was also a skilled teacher.

Many of us, including myself, had rarely been close to a horse. Rosie's attitude and example made it clear that riding a horse was the easiest thing in the world. I wasn't so easily convinced. I had admired the horses as we drove into the ranch for the first time, and had seen them from the windows almost every day. Now I was expected to groom, clean up after and ride them. The last thing I wanted was to get filthy hanging around with horses, but I didn't want Rosie to think I was a chicken.

The time spent with the horses lasted two and a half hours, and by the end of the first day, despite my best efforts, I was sweating, dusty and smelly. There had been no good way to clean up other than a quick rinse at the water tap. I couldn't control the impression I made. People who maybe hadn't seen the oozing sores beneath my life's surface could now certainly see the similar coating on the outside. It made me crazy, yet the animal lover inside was reluctant to leave. After that first session, I was hooked. My horse's name was Teddy Ears, and I wanted to stay even longer, talking to him and gazing into those fathomless brown eyes that looked at me so patiently.

My constant fear of looking stupid in front of others was quickly uncovered as I rode. I bounced, slid and shook all the way around the riding arena. Afraid to go fast, because I might fall off and look stupid, I poked along trying to do everything right. One day, embarrassed at being left behind, I spurred my horse into a canter. Heart pounding, I tried to remember how to stay in the saddle. Rosie watched with amusement, then amazement, as my horse and I found our stride and did lap after lap around her.

I pulled off my hat, threw it in the air and screamed, "Look at me! I'm so proud of myself I could just spit!" Everyone laughed and applauded, and that day I left the stables dirty and happy and proud. It was a breakthrough. I was conquering fear. I was also conquering perfectionism. Only a few weeks before, I couldn't have stood to have filthy hands and dirt under my fingernails. Now I considered it a good trade for getting to spend time at the stable.

When we were proficient enough in the saddle, we took trail rides into the desert. It was early spring and the cactus was beginning to bloom. No buildings were visible once we got out a little way from headquarters, and it was blessedly tranquil. Led by Rosie or one of her staff, serenity stole into our hearts as we covered mile after dusty mile.

In the desert, the ground looks like gritty dirt from a distance or at a casual glance. But if you look closely, mixed in with the soil are glints of light and color—pieces of quartz that work their way to the surface or are broken from larger pieces. Milky white or pale pink, they are beautiful. Trail rides were my sparkling quartz in the dirt of therapy. I had never considered horses a tool of therapy, but they worked their magic with me.

Equine Therapy became my favorite activity, and the horses became my great friends, enduring all the affection I doled out so carefully to members of the human race. The horses didn't judge me, and I felt no need to prove myself to them. Each day after riding, as I walked back up the hill from the stable to the main lodge, I felt relaxed and confident.

And amazingly—I felt hungry.

Learning to Trust

Forget the former things; do not dwell on the past. See, I am doing a new thing! Now it springs up; do you not perceive it? I am making a way in the desert and streams in the wasteland.

—Isaiah 43:18-19

As I sat in Process Group during my first week of treatment, listening to others talk about memories and hurts, little doors began to open and shut in my mind. I would experience a glimpse from the past; then it would be gone. I had a brief vision of little Sandy, six years old, crawling to the back of the bathroom closet and being pulled out and beaten. Then as I grew older, mental pictures of someone leaning over me, rubbing me in a private place as I tried to sleep. Horrible memories of young adult years, being drunk and intimate with men. The past swirled around me, becoming angry and demanding. My chest burned and hurt, and I felt as though it would burst.

Don asked me to describe how I was feeling. I said it felt like I had a bowling ball in my chest. When he asked me to try to give the feeling a name, guilt was the only word I could come up with, though it didn't feel exactly right. After a few moments, he very gently suggested the word *shame.*

The power of the word overwhelmed me. I felt my emotions beginning to swell against the door I had kept so carefully guarded through the years. *Shame.* I never would have suspected the impact applying this word to my past would have on me. I felt bad and dirty about all of the things I was beginning to remember. Shame crushed my heart with a weight so heavy that it hurt. Shame squeezed my lungs until it seemed I couldn't breathe. For years I had been operating in total self-blame and recrimination.

Don talked a little about shame, and how patients tend to have taken on the self-hatred associated with it even when they had not committed the sin. The things that happened to me when I was a child were not my choice or my fault, he said.

My feelings confused me. How could I not be bad? All my life, I had viewed events I experienced as extensions of myself, assuming the things that had happened to me were things I should have been able to control. I became very self-centered, blaming myself for everything.

I Didn't Tell My Daddy Good-bye

In my mind, I drifted to the past. It was the spring of 1960, the year I turned three. Though I was very young, I carry a memory of that time for it marked the event which set in motion a struggle within me, one which would haunt me all my life: the battle between wanting to be loved and not believing that I deserved to be loved.

My sister Debbie and I were playing when Mom came and said that we must get ready to get in the car. Daddy's chest hurt, and we had to take him to the hospital. Once in the car in the front seat with Mom, we realized that Daddy was very sick. He lay on the back seat, and his face was gray. At the hospital, men came and took him away. Now I was scared. A lady in a pink dress came to the car with coloring books and candy.

Hours later, my grandmother came and took us to her house. When the news finally came, she sat us on her bed and told us that Daddy had gone to heaven to live with Jesus. I thought it was mean that he wouldn't come back, and wondered whether he was mad at me. Mee-Maw said that Daddy could not come back, but if we loved Jesus and obeyed Him, we could go to live with Daddy and Him some day. I saw a picture in my mind of a bright, blue sky and fluffy white clouds. I was searching for a wooden ladder reaching up through the clouds that I figured must be there. I wanted to climb to heaven to see my daddy, but I could not.

I was three, and my daddy had died. One day he was there, teasing me to get me to eat my asparagus, and then the next day he was gone. After the men took him away at that hospital emergency room, I never saw him again. We were not allowed to go to the funeral, because in those days people considered it harmful for children to be exposed to death. I never had a chance to tell my daddy good-bye.

Mom then put all of Daddy's things away and didn't talk about him much after that. Our house looked different without him. I remember wishing that I could smell his after-shave again. At such a young age, I was too young to understand that Mom was being counseled to deal with her grief by being strong for her girls and not to let us see her cry or sense her fear. All I knew was that my beloved daddy was gone and my whole world had changed.

The most important man in my life had abandoned me. Every morning he kissed us good-bye before he went to work and every afternoon we walked to the bus stop to meet him. Seeing him was a highlight of every day. Was he gone because of something I had done? I don't know if I really blamed myself then for his death, although I remember feeling very afraid.

Mom had to get a job and we had to move to another apartment. It was 1960, and difficult to be a single parent. She had a hard time finding a place for us to live because no one wanted to rent to a single mother with two children. The apartment we finally settled in was an upper flat with wooden floors. Debbie and I had to be very quiet and not run around so we wouldn't disturb the tenant below us. We went to an older woman's house while Mom worked.

Mom remarried within a year of Daddy's death. My sister and I were thrilled. We wanted a new daddy so badly. Our stepfather had a nice house on an acre of land with a creek in the backyard. He had a son and daughter from a previous marriage and we were excited to have a big brother and sister. We went to the drive-in movies in his station wagon, and when we got home, I would pretend to be asleep so that he would carry me inside.

Our new dad had a great sense of humor, and loved to tease. I loved it when he played Bill Cosby records. My step dad would imitate him and we would all laugh. But he also had a bad temper and he was very scary when he was angry. Mom told me that I must obey my stepfather, and if I didn't I would be spanked.

I had some very definite ideas about rules I would obey and those I would not, and as a result I was spanked often and hard. Because I was spanked for things that didn't seem bad to me, it reinforced my belief that I was no good. I began to resent my stepfather for spanking me and Mom for not stopping him.

Longing for Love

I feared but loved my stepfather, and I wanted him to be my daddy. He told Debbie and me to call him by his first name, not Daddy. Hating this, I started calling him Pop, because that's what he called his dad. At the time, I had no way of knowing why he was reluctant to father me in a close and nurturing way. I wanted to sit on his lap and cuddle. I wanted to be special to him. But Pop was awkward in his expressions of love towards us, his newly adopted daughters, which made his attempts at affection few and far between.

One moment in my childhood stands out. I was in second grade. I awoke to the sound of Pop's voice calling me out of a deep sleep, saying, "Wake up, Princess. "It's Valentine's Day and you have a very pretty dress to wear to your party." It was a moment I cherished. How I longed to have it repeated every day.

As the years went on I clowned and misbehaved to get attention. As a result, most of the attention I got was negative. It began to dawn on me that something must be wrong with me. I just wasn't very lovable or surely Pop would love me. All these memories and feelings were collecting in my consciousness, and I was becoming even more confused.

No Easy Fix

Going through the motions of daily activity at the ranch, I was overwhelmed more and more each day by past memories. Memories that hurt. Feeling like a little girl with no protection, I realized that there was no easy or quick fix for my eating disorder. I also began to understand that these glimpses from my childhood were part of my present pain and behavior. Yet seeing connections between my past and present didn't make the process any easier. It didn't seem possible that merely talking about hurtful experiences could change the way I felt as an adult. So many memories and feelings were surfacing and competing for attention, it seemed impossible to deal with them all.

My favorite coping mechanisms of humor and pretending helped me deal with my growing confusion and fear. I joked with the other patients and therapists and tried to look thoughtful when it seemed inappropriate to smile. Staff immediately saw the signs of someone retreating into herself, and encouraged me to share my struggle with them. By then I trusted Don enough to tell him that I was overwhelmed by the enormity of the task before me. I didn't see how 31 years of confusion and pain could be resolved in just a few months. He reassured me that I wasn't expected to completely figure myself out during my stay at the Ranch. I could begin to identify my problems and deal with the symptoms of bulimia while I was there, and I could continue the process of healing once I returned to my home in Wisconsin.

A journal entry from January 28, 1990, expresses the turmoil I was beginning to feel. "The task ahead seems easy yet hard. Easy because I know now what has to be done, hard because I don't want to do it. I'm tired of hurting, and from what I hear, it hurts worse to get it out. The feelings have been stuffed, kept inside for so long that they've intensified—I see them as bigger and more powerful than they are."

God began to show His grace and love to me in a very personal way. I was beginning to grasp the magnitude of the task before me. I had to start "sorting my laundry." The huge emotional sack I had dragged everywhere was the key to my recovery and freedom. Every item in it had to be removed, examined and put in its place. Was I carrying that item and its pain because someone had sinned against me and I blamed myself for their actions? Some of the laundry might be my own sin that I believed God could not forgive. I had no idea where to start. It seemed that He had brought me here and revealed a task to me that I couldn't accomplish. Why was I in this place? All of this pain and ugliness had been revealed, with no plan or promises for resolving it.

One morning before breakfast, Patty was reading her Bible and praying. I wanted to look busy and spiritual, so I sat in our room with my Bible, too. Not knowing what to read, I asked God, the only real father I'd known, for hope. Looking up "hope" in the concordance led me to Romans 8:24-25: "But hope that is seen is no hope at all. Who hopes for what he already has? But if we hope for what we do not yet have, we wait for it patiently."

I prayed that somehow God would give me the patience I needed to get through treatment. "God," I said, "I know that You don't give advice when I open my Bible, close my eyes and put my finger on a page. I don't know where to look in Your Word, but I need some specific encouragement." Nothing came to me as I flipped through the pages. I was getting discouraged, but I was sure that I looked industrious to anyone watching.

A Way in the Desert

Paging through the Old Testament, I stopped at the book of Isaiah. I'd never spent much time in that part of the Bible. Prophecy seemed beyond my comprehension, and I found Jewish law and genealogy dull. I skimmed the pages, and my eyes fell on chapter 43, verses 18 and 19: "Forget the former things; do not dwell on the past. See, I am doing a new thing! Now it springs up; do you not perceive it? I am making a way in the desert and streams in the wasteland."

My heart leaped. This was it! I had traveled many miles to the desert, and I certainly was a wasteland! God had brought me to this place to do a new thing in my life. I had asked Him for reassurance, and He gave it to me. Feeling grateful and more positive, I determined to get to work and face my past one day at a time.

I had now been hospitalized for two weeks. It was obvious that the work had just begun and that I would need to extend my stay at the treatment center. In the coming days, Isaiah 43:18-19 began to make even more sense. The therapists made it clear to me that before I could "forget" or put aside former things I first had to remember them. In order not to dwell on my past, I had to forgive those who had hurt me, ask forgiveness of those whom I had hurt and, most importantly, accept God's forgiveness for myself.

I had thought that when I accepted Christ as my Savior, all of the painful things in my past would cease to matter and that the pain would go away. At my moment of salvation, I had prayed a blanket prayer for forgiveness of my past sins. I didn't realize that I also had to let go of those hurts and sins before they would no longer affect my life. That entailed specifically revisiting painful moments in my life, and I was finally ready to get down to business. Until I did the hard work, I couldn't leave my messy bag of emotional laundry at the foot of the cross and walk away free of my past.

Deck Chairs on the Titanic

They scurried frantically around polishing and straightening, getting everything perfect for the maiden voyage. They were the fated stewards, arranging deck chairs on the Titanic.

—Sue Govier

Moving into the third week of treatment, I began to notice that the other patients were making progress. They were able to talk about their pain in therapy, and their attitudes about food were changing.

As an anorexic, Patty had a very hard time convincing herself that food is a blessing. For so many years, she had seen it as her enemy, something to make her fat. Now she tickled us by visualizing her meals as wrapped gifts from God. She made an index card to keep at her place at the table that read, *This food is a special present from God. It is good for me and I am thankful for it.* Before she ate, she would mentally go through the process of untying a ribbon and removing wrapping paper from her plate. It was a very creative way of transforming her attitudes about eating.

I began to allow myself to hope that I could open up about my past and learn how to enjoy food without feeling guilty. Looking at the other women there, I saw very lovable people who had problems and pain. I listened to my new friends talk about the abuse and rejection in their lives, and was glad that I didn't have to feel as bad as they seemed to.

Ironically, as I empathized with their experiences and anguish, it was becoming more difficult for me to express my own. I would hear someone express an emotion related to something or someone that had hurt them, and I would feel a tug in my own heart. I began to feel the same feelings, but immediately pushed them down. Their pain snagged mine, and I was afraid.

When Sarah talked about how angry and sad she was when her dad moved out, I had a fleeting thought of my own daddy and I began to feel sad, too. I feared that if I allowed myself to dwell on the emotion, memories would seep through the protective barrier I had built around my heart—the wall that kept me safe and shielded me from pain that I feared would quickly get out of control. I was almost more afraid of the feelings themselves than what was behind them. In order to find out what was behind them, I would have to feel the feeling, and I could not do that. When feelings came, my armpits got damp. I felt hot and had a hard time breathing. Lightheaded and nauseous, I pushed the feelings back where they could not frighten me.

The wall around my heart had functions I wasn't aware of. It kept my emotions and memories away from me, but it also separated me from others, including God. For years I wondered why I didn't feel as close to God as I wanted. As a born-again Christian, my personal relationship with Christ was supposed to be the most important thing in my life.

However, the feelings I ran from and my addiction were really my top priority. It was something else to feel guilty about, and I assumed I was so bad that He couldn't be close to me. Unknown to me, all the time Jesus was patiently waiting outside the wall around my heart.

Spiritual Growth group began to shed some light on the issue of intimacy with God. In it, we examined what God was revealing to us, and our responses to the hurtful events at the time they occurred. The group leader introduced a brand-new concept to me called "vows and judgments." I didn't know that when I judged someone's motives or behaviors and vowed to not be like them, I was setting myself up. Much later I would find those hurtful tendencies in myself. People had hurt me, and I was beginning to recognize the people and the events. But how had I responded to the pain? As a child, I felt that there was no one to protect me, so I protected myself by judging the ones who hurt me. I would avoid anything that made me appear to be like them.

Reaping What I Sowed

Without knowing it, I was violating a principle set down in God's Word long ago. Jesus illustrated the fertile soil of our heart in Mark 4:26-27: "This is what the kingdom of God is like. A man scatters seed on the ground. Night and day, whether he sleeps or gets up, the seed sprouts and grows, though he does not know how.'" I was the ground and my judgments were the seeds. Thinking about my wounds and dreaming about what I would like to say to those who had hurt me felt good. Ignorant of His ways and protecting myself in my own childish ways, I began to sow seeds of bitterness in my heart. In my mind, I decided they were bad and went over and over their offenses, vowing that

I would never be like them. I would never hurt anyone the way they had hurt me.

I determined that I would never be like my parents. I hated the men who sexually abused me, and swore in my heart never to be completely vulnerable with a man. Brick by brick I built a wall around my heart, designed to keep me safe from harm. In due course, I became a suspicious, defensive woman. Convinced that everyone was out to get me, I saw danger where there was none. Any injury, real or imagined, resulted in my adding another brick to my fortress. On the outside I was the life of the party—witty, silly and desperately wanting people to love me. On the inside, I was wounded and scared. I hunkered behind my wall, determined to protect myself, reasoning that if I never fully exposed myself, no one could hurt me. Consequently, even my closest friends didn't know the real me.

The seeds of bitterness I sowed beginning in childhood grew to maturity and bore bitter fruit. I had never wanted to be spiteful, hateful or full of pride, but all were festering in my heart, covered up by a charming Christian mask. I was very adept at verbally ripping my husband to shreds any time I perceived a threat. I shamed my children to get the behavior I wanted. Lies were the fruit of my mistrust.

As a Christian, I believed that all of this was appalling and unacceptable. My life became an exercise in plucking bitter fruit, praying for forgiveness but watching with shame and dismay as, like a weed in a garden, it grew back. In treatment I was discovering why I harvested in my life the very things I hated in others. I had violated basic scriptural principles, and was reaping what I had sown.

This information astounded me. For the first time, I understood how my past affected my present. I could clearly see the cause and effect of my actions and the actions of others. I also began to sense that recovery wasn't just about getting over an eating disorder, but about deep heart-change. Merely remembering events wasn't enough. I had to want to let God change my heart, to begin to heal the anger and shame I harbored.

Spiritual Growth was about changing my heart, and Process Group was all about remembering events and identifying the feelings that were associated with what had happened. Sitting on a couch in a comfortable room with the sun slanting in the windows, what I wanted most was to run away from what was beginning to emerge in my heart and mind. I had been closed to feelings for so long, it was exhausting to access them.

Violent Vision from the Past

This day in Process Group, Patty was talking about being raped as a teenager and her inability to tell her mother. She had been frightened, and had nowhere to turn. Listening to her, I began to have difficulty breathing. My stomach hurt and I couldn't sit still. I crossed my legs and hugged a large pillow to my chest.

Don asked me to tell the group what I was thinking and feeling, but the words would not come. Again, I was seeing my teenage face in the bathroom mirror in my childhood home. Fighting nausea, I said that I felt like Patty, and he asked me to tell him and the group why. The weight of shame nearly crushed me, and I could barely speak. A weird image of the past surfaced. I had been a different person then. I bit my nails and I was much heavier. I didn't like to remember that girl. But a terrifying event of the past was unfolding before me as though it was happening again.

It was 1975, my senior year in high school. I was 17, and working in a pet store at the mall. It was closing time, and I was in the back room, alone in the store. Closing entailed feeding the animals and cleaning their cages, vacuuming and making a deposit of receipts from the cash register. I loved that part of the day because it gave me an opportunity to play with the animals. My favorite was "Hans," a trained chimpanzee that I let follow me around the store as I went about my tasks. When I was nearly done, I noticed that one of the large aquariums in the back room was leaking. Sighing, I scooped Hans up so he wouldn't play in the water, and as I carried him to his cage, I said, "I guess I'll have to call John"—my boss, the store manager.

I really didn't want to call John because he seemed to enjoy making me uncomfortable by talking about sexual things. I was a virgin, and very inexperienced sexually. The thought of being alone in the store with him when the mall was closed was scary, so I called the assistant manager. She said I'd have to call the manager because she wasn't sure how to deal with the aquarium problem either.

Reluctantly, I dialed his home number and explained the problem. He was there in just a few minutes, and we transferred the fish to another tank, emptied the water out of the broken one and cleaned up the mess on the floor. As usual, John talked about my body as we worked. Not wanting to anger him, I said nothing. Suddenly, my back was against the office wall and he was begging me to have sex. I said No and pushed him away, heading for the doorway and freedom into the mall.

However, he attacked me and threw me down. I hit the floor so hard, I was dazed. Then he was on top of me, his forearm over my mouth and his other hand tearing at my jeans. He said that if I screamed, the only ones to hear would be the mall maintenance men and he would tell them that we did this all the time.

Afterward, in the store's bathroom, I felt sick and trapped. I wanted to call my mom to come and get me because I didn't think I could drive home. When I came out, John was waiting. He said that he was going to take me home, and that if I told my parents anything about what had happened, he would tell them that we had been having sex for months and that they would believe him.

He was probably right. Mom never believed anything I told her. We fought constantly about where I had been and what I was doing. Convinced that my parents had no right to boss me around, I frequently lied to them in order to avoid trouble when I broke curfew or other house rules. Not surprisingly, they didn't trust me. All the way home, John told me how humiliated I would be if I cried "Rape!" and my friends found out that I was no longer the little virgin they thought I was. Who would want to date me? By the time we got to my house, I was defeated.

Putting on a normal face, I told my parents that I was late because I'd had car trouble and my boss had given me a ride. Then I went into the bathroom and leaned over the sink. Sick and filled with self-loathing, I looked into the mirror. My face was an image that would haunt me all of my life. Pale, frightened and ashamed that my precious virginity had been taken from me, I felt I was ruined.

Although I felt cornered by all this, I realized while lying awake that night that the worst hadn't occurred yet. What if I were to get pregnant? Who could I tell? None of my friends were sophisticated enough to help me figure this one out. After a sleepless night, I called my mom into my room and told her what had happened. She was shocked. Had I wanted to have sex with him? At my angry denial, she said she would call the doctor, and left my room. I know now that what I thought was anger and disgust in her manner and voice was in fact shock. Mom wasn't any better prepared for this crisis than was I.

I saw the doctor, had a painfully embarrassing examination, was questioned and then given a prescription for a pill that would prevent me from getting pregnant. My parents decided not to go to the police because everyone would find out about the rape. The neighbors and members of our church would know. Kids at school would talk. We were a private family and kept our business hidden from others. A veil of secrecy was drawn over my rape. The subject was dropped, and I felt totally abandoned and alone.

Sorority of Suffering

Telling about my experience 14 years later in the group, all I felt was shame. I couldn't meet anyone's eyes. Not until later would I realize the love and compassion that radiated from the group members. Each one identified in my story some private hurt which they had also held in secret. I expressed how alone I had felt, and how sure I was that my parents thought I had given away my virginity. As an adult many years later, I still felt alone.

Later, in another session of Process Group, I told about other excruciating experiences that scarred me. In separate instances when I was between nine and 12, I was inappropriately touched and kissed by men in my family who had a responsibility to protect and love me. It felt offensive, and I sensed that it was wrong. Afraid to tell anyone about these episodes, I believed that their actions were punishment for some unnamed misbehavior of mine. It seemed that I was constantly in trouble for my conduct. In my child's mind, I decided that I must be very wicked to behave so badly that these men wanted to discipline me so harshly. That belief followed me into adulthood.

Even now, it's hard to describe the feelings I had toward myself. I felt full of despair, convinced that my character was hopelessly flawed. My life became an exercise in building and maintaining a perfect mask. The brown ooze must never show. No one could possibly be as bad as I. At whatever cost, I must look perfect. Murky and dark, my past was firmly shut behind a door in the basement of my soul. I never wanted to look inside, for it was too ugly.

Sometimes, however, I would find myself remembering, seeing dim outlines of evils from my past. Bouts of drunkenness taunted me from the shadows of long ago. There was my stepfather's anger and my mother's frustration as she tried to build a bridge between us. Lies I had told and relationships I had manipulated…a marriage that lasted eight months in college…hateful words and actions used in defense—all this and more lurked near the edge of my consciousness, memories that were stored in the basement of my mind.

Packed away in the farthest, darkest corner of my secret hiding place were memories of sexual relationships I had entered into in a desperate search for love. I ignored them, pretended not to care and blamed them on the permissiveness of the decade in which I had grown up. I thought I had contained these shameful memories, but they were too powerful to remain hidden. Leaking around and under the locked door of my soul, they were the brown ooze I so desperately fought to hide.

This was the room in my soul that I had not allowed even Jesus to enter. A blanket prayer for forgiveness of sins, then I had slapped a sturdy lock on the door. How could God still love me if I showed Him those things? I knew God was there through all of the sinful attempts to dull the pain that followed me, but I was ignorant of His grace. I pretended He didn't see and convinced myself that He must not care, hoping He would take away the pain and the craving for love.

Even when I finally tired of my sin and turned to God, I couldn't open my secret basement's door. Surely even He couldn't love me after the things I had done. Hiding behind my mask, I pretended my basement didn't exist, while my soul yawned with emptiness nothing could fill.

My life was an exercise in pretending nothing was wrong while looking for something or someone to make me feel better. I instinctively believed that if I put on a front good enough for someone to love me, my secrets would stay hidden and my hunger would be satisfied.

Outer Changes, Inner Pain

In 1981, I married again and pledged to become a better person, to make myself worthy of God's forgiveness and my husband's love. I would keep my soul's basement locked up tight, and eventually I would forget what was hidden there.

Changing the outward behaviors of alcohol abuse and promiscuity was relatively easy. I belonged to one man now, and I was faithful. Drinking didn't fit into my new image for myself of a married Christian woman. Outwardly I had changed, but inside, my self-loathing continued to simmer.

Terrified my husband would discover my past and see me for the ugly, unlovable person I was, I desperately cast about for a better mask—and an escape from the pain that still tormented me. Striving for excellence in my job as an Air Force officer wasn't enough. I lived in fear my incompetence would be discovered, even though my performance ratings were very high. Finally I took refuge in the one thing I was sure would secure Scott's love and acceptance: my appearance. It was the perfect disguise. As long as I looked good on the outside, he would have no reason to look beneath the surface. He wouldn't discover my ugliness, and he would always love me.

The only area of my appearance I felt I could control was my weight. I quit eating except for two small meals a day. In two months, I dropped almost 30 pounds. Everyone, including Scott, told me how great I looked, and I knew I had found the answer. As hunger became my focus, the emotional pain receded.

Because I had found a new way to dull the pain, it became possible to shut the door to the basement of my past with all its hurts. Now, all these years later, the honesty of other women in treatment with me, and the efforts of a persistent and loving staff, prompted me to open the door and explore my most private pain. In individual and group sessions, I entered my soul's basement, the place where I had desperately tried to contain the ooze. Gradually, God's light was shed on experiences and events I had hoped never to see again.

I would soon see that trying to appear perfect was, like arranging deck chairs on the Titanic, futile in the face of the storm that was to come.

Behind the Mask

He who would distinguish the true from the false must have an idea of what is true and what is false.

—Benedict Spinoza, 1632–1677

As my past was being revealed, feelings began to emerge with the memories. Anger, fear, sadness and loneliness were chief among them. I had come to believe that these feelings were bad. No one, I was certain, liked a little girl or woman who is mad or who cries. I had learned to push the feelings deep inside myself and ignore them.

Self-control, however, only went so far in controlling my emotions. All my life I had episodes when I could no longer keep a lid on ugly passions. I could only stuff them down for a while, then I would erupt into fits of screaming and crying that frightened everyone. I couldn't forgive myself after those episodes. My behavior had been inappropriate, and I was afraid of what those who witnessed it must be thinking of me.

Now that fear also applied to the staff at the Ranch. Seeing glimmers of hope that I could recover from my eating disorder was one thing. Being willing to allow myself to feel and display the full force of the pain attached to emerging memories was something else.

A Stirring of Monsters

Two weeks into treatment, my ability to cover up began to weaken. As I realized that I had to remember, understand and feel a lifetime of suppressed pain, my defenses became vulnerable. I had been smiling and denying for so long that I really didn't know how to allow myself to feel. A smile had been my shield for most of my life. It protected me from the scrutiny of others, and it kept the aching in my heart and soul confined. Now my protective walls were crumbling. The sleeping monsters in my basement were beginning to stir. Like a pressure cooker untended, I was ready to blow.

A lifetime of feelings was trapped inside. Bulimia and angry outbursts at my husband and kids had relieved the pressure in the past. Now, however, I couldn't binge and purge, and I was afraid that if I allowed myself to feel even a little, the results would be catastrophic. I would explode and the full force of anger, sadness and pain would kill me.

All through my adult life I experienced intense moments of passion that scared me. It might be anger, fear, sadness or occasionally joy, but whatever the emotion I was frightened by how strongly I felt it. At various times I had hurled coffee cups and shoes (once through a picture window), screamed at people, kicked holes in doors, punched holes in drywall—and once I bit someone. Those things happened while I was restraining myself! I always repressed the feelings as much as possible because I didn't know what would happen if I let go. Deep down inside I was really mad at just about everything, but I had been raised to believe that people liked me better when I was happy. My anger had always been rewarded with discipline, so I fumed inside and smiled on the outside.

Even in a place where my life was laid bare, I couldn't release my grip on the smiling mask I showed to others. To do so was to risk being rejected by the people around me. The very thought of exposure was worse than the thought of my feelings overwhelming me. I really didn't know what was acceptable to feel and express. While I was beginning to understand that I had to face some hard and hurtful things, I stubbornly held onto my smile and my standard answer of "fine" whenever someone asked me how I was feeling. They still didn't know about the brown ooze, and I wasn't going to let them see it.

My nails were looking better and my knuckles less scraped, now that I wasn't shoving them down my throat every day. I told myself that I could get over the desire to binge and purge without showing anyone the real me. Don, my therapist, knew that I was holding back, and he took every opportunity to remind me that honesty was the key to getting well.

I was beginning to wonder if there was enough time in the world to begin to sort out my spiritual and emotional mess. Yet I believed that God wanted me well and that Jesus had died on the cross so I might have a full, healthy life. Part of my task while in treatment was to identify how I had been spiritually and emotionally wounded. Staff told me that once I knew how I had been hurt and what harmful choices I had made, I could begin to do the work necessary to heal.

A Crisis of Faith

Having it laid out like a blueprint in front of me made the whole process seem much more doable. The problem was that my church had taught me that *my* part was to believe and have faith that God would heal me, and it would be done. If it were true that I should be healed by faith alone, then was I a bad Christian because I was bulimic and depressed? Probably. If my faith was inadequate, then it was my fault that I was sick. I would be healed if I had greater faith, or so I thought.

Obviously I wasn't healed, and I began to have a crisis of faith. Here in treatment they were telling me to allow faith to give me the courage to walk through the painful process of forgiving others and to ask God to forgive me for my mistakes. With staff's assurances that I could survive and heal, I was willing to open some of my old wounds. However, my stay was projected to be about 90 days, and I was afraid that by then I would just be getting started pulling the scabs off of my heart. The thought of going home with every raw nerve in my soul exposed was terrifying.

I struggled to determine how much ooze to release and how much to hide. My goal was to get well without having to "let it all hang out." Somehow I felt that I had to hang on to a few secrets. There were some very unacceptable things in my past, and I felt sure that not even the other bruised souls in this treatment center could love me if they found out. As a Christian, I thought I knew that there were rules, even for painful pasts. I wanted to be a socially acceptable Christian victim/patient, and to do this, I felt I needed to retain control over how much of myself I revealed.

It was the second day of trying to come to terms not only with my spiritual crisis, but also the memories that were emerging in group therapy. I was eating dinner when my therapist, Don, paused by my table on his way out for the night. He asked me how I was feeling. Feeling truly awful, I smiled and said yet again, "Fine."

Don's reply was, "Drop your smiling mask, Sandy. It must get awfully heavy"—and he left. I was devastated. As depressed as I was feeling, just eating seemed like a huge task. Pretending was the only way I thought I could get through the meal.

Suddenly, fury took over. I refused to eat, stormed away from the table, went to my room and slammed the door. Shaking and sweating, I wanted to break something. My fear of looking like a fool took a back seat to the anger I couldn't contain. What did Don think he was doing? How dare he jerk away my only defense? Nice people were supposed to smile and not burden others with their troubles!

It had been years since I had allowed myself to feel so angry. Unable to express it verbally, and afraid that I would quickly get out of control, I collapsed on the couch. The anger drained away and was replaced with despair. Totally confused and utterly dejected, I wanted to die. Nothing seemed clear. Was faith the answer, or did I have to give up all of my defenses and expose myself completely before I could get well?

A Soul's Dark Night

I spent four hours lying in my room without speaking. I couldn't express in words the blackness that surrounded me. All of the rejection, abandonment, loneliness and fear I had ever known engulfed me. I had just begun to trust some of the treatment staff, and now I could trust no one. Suddenly I understood why they had gone through my luggage so thoroughly when I was admitted. If I had had the means to kill myself, I would have done it. I didn't know how I was going to get well, and I couldn't go home. All hope was lost.

It was the darkest night my soul had ever experienced. I felt that I could trust no human being. I had no means of killing myself, so death wasn't an option. Finally, the mental health technician I had chosen to trust came and sat on the arm of the couch. She began to explain that some of the others at the center had also been in a place of no hope. Without God's healing, these same people, now my friends, would not have been there at that moment, offering me hope and encouragement.

That night, the words of a song based on Psalm 27 met me at my point of deepest need: "All I desire of the Lord is to seek His face and dwell in His tent forever." That was all I desired, too, but everything seemed muddy. My relationship with God had never been clear, even in the best times. I knew that I was saved, but felt I had let God down so many times, I was barely worthy to be called His child. I felt undeserving of His love, and my faith was weak. Yet, although I was afraid, I clung that night to the words of that song, and asked God to allow me into His tent.

The next day Don and I sat at a table at the end of the lawn outside the main building. It overlooked the stables, with the mountains in the background. The sun was warm, and I was wary. We had to talk about my feeling of exposure. I was angry with him for pulling at my mask the night before. Bruised in spirit, I tried to tell him how angry I was without getting mad. I did not want to express anger, for I had learned to associate anger with pain—sometimes physical pain.

As I struggled, a scene from my teen years played through my mind. It was 1974 and I was 16. Mom and I were arguing. Again. Overcome with emotion, and helpless to express it, I screamed, "I hate you!" Her eyes filled with tears, her face crumpled, and I ran from the room. My stepfather angrily followed me down the hall to my room, jerked open the door and shouted that I would not talk to my mother that way. The battle continued, now with him.

Another memory filtered through, this time from a brief and failing marriage I had entered into in 1978 at the age of

20. My first husband leaned into my face, screaming at me. The sharp edge of the cabinet in the tiny bathroom pushed into my back. I screamed back, and he wrenched my arm, twisting it behind my back, and pushed me into the tub. So angry that I wasn't afraid of getting hurt, I lurched out of the tub, still shrieking, and began swinging at him. I never connected. When his first blow hit me in the side of the head, fear struck, too. My anger dissolved, and I begin to cry and ran out of the apartment and down the stairs.

I told Don that I was angry with him for so abruptly pulling at my mask. At the same time I was desperately afraid. I didn't know that anger didn't have to be homicidal or destructive. I had so many years of anger stuffed down inside me that my reactions to it were way out of proportion. Situations that merited mere irritation received instead the full force of all of my anger. I didn't know that once the anger inside me was expressed, discussed and prayed about, it would begin to dissipate. Then I could be angry and still be reasonable, dealing with each feeling as it arose.

I could have fled to any number of places to avoid Don's reaction to my anger that day. But 30 years had taught me that no matter where I went, the results of my anger went with me. With eyes full of tears and lip trembling, I looked down at my hands in my lap and waited. My anger was an ugly, dark shape without much definition. We sat there in silence for a long moment.

A Safe Place for Anger

Then, with compassion, Don told me that I had a right to be angry—with him and with many others in my life. Gently he talked about the pain I had suffered as a little girl, hurts from which my parents could have protected me. Many of the terrible memories I had from my teen years were punctuated by the anguish of knowing that there was no one by my side to fight for me and shelter me from harm. At that time I didn't know why I had had no protection. As an adult, I had no concept of protection other than anger and running—or a smiling face that gave no one reason to hurt me.

The ad that I had seen for this treatment center had described it as a safe environment. I thought that meant that they locked the doors at night. Don explained it meant that I could express any feeling and not get hurt. No one there would shame me, laugh at me or abandon me. Like seeing a light gradually brightening, I realized I'd never known a place where I could honestly and safely express my emotions.

Relief washed over me as Don told me how angry he was that my parents hadn't assured me that they believed I had been raped. Had I looked up in group, after telling the story, I would have seen compassion on the faces of the other patients as they pictured me alone, hurt and frightened, with no one to comfort me. He assured me that this was safety; I could feel and express all of my anger at the rapist and my family. Staff would be there to support me. They wouldn't let my anger get so out of control that anyone would get hurt. I began to feel hope as my therapist told me the best news. Everyone here would still love and accept me when my anger was spent.

Finally I could see that I had allowed my need to keep my disguise in place to drive me to a point very near death. For far too long, I had struggled vainly to keep up appearances.

It had been nearly five weeks. My smiling mask had finally been torn away.

Truth in Love

So it is more useful to watch a man in times of peril, and in adversity to discern what kind of man he is; for then at last words of truth are drawn from the depths of his heart, and the mask is torn off, reality remains.

—De Rerum Natura, Book III, l. 55

Family Week is the part of the treatment process that brings the patient together with the people who are most important to her. Since eating disorders are more about feelings than food, the people linked to the patient's emotions play a significant part in her recovery. Often a patient's wounds stem from her childhood. When those wounds have manifested themselves in an eating disorder, a large part of recovery is openly discussing those early incidents and allowing everyone involved to gain insight and work toward forgiveness and closure.

The goals of Family Week are honesty expressed in love, forgiveness, understanding and healing. Its purpose is never to place blame. Family members learn about eating disorders, they are given a safe place to discuss their own feelings and communication is fostered between them and their loved ones.

Most patients' families arrive for Family Week nervous and unprepared. For many, this is their first experience with therapy of any kind. Usually they know very little about eating disorders, and are confused about how they fit into the picture. In some cases, as in mine, parents, husbands and children know nothing about the patient's eating disorder until the need for hospitalization exposes it.

A Scary Step into Reality

A "truth in love" list is given to each patient to fill out at the beginning of Family Week. It is a tool used to list and define the issues we will discuss with our families. Completing a sheet for each of the people who had the greatest influence in my life (my mother, stepfather and my husband, Scott) was a scary step into the reality of how I felt toward each of them.

The emotional tangle of my life had become more clear to me during the time I had been at the ranch. By now, the one thing I did know was that a lot of different feelings were anxiously waiting for expression, lined up like homeless souls at a soup kitchen, desperate for release from their hunger. Revealing many years of unspoken, unacknowledged bumps and bruises had left me very fearful that Family Week would shatter my life and I would be alone. This fear was at the root of a hurt that had driven my choices for many years.

I had been told for six weeks that acknowledging and voicing my emotions was crucial to getting well. Still, years of conditioning had seared into me the belief that one did not expose the family's dirty laundry. I felt strongly that my parents would leave furious with me for talking about my childhood. Instead of improving our relationship, I feared that Family Week would result in complete rejection.

My turn with family therapy did not come until late in the week. By then I had observed my friends face their families, with varying outcomes. No one was mean or horribly angry. Some achieved complete forgiveness right away, and some admitted that they had a long way to go. All, however, confirmed their love for one another.

I spent the first part of the week imagining the worst. What if we were the first family to lose it and leave hating each other? I knew that I had some significant anger to express, and I could only guess at what my parents had to say to me. By the time my day came, I was a mess. I didn't want to eat, but had to. So nervous that I had diarrhea, I just hoped I could make it through the entire session without having to run for the bathroom.

There was a short break before my session began, and I took a brief walk to pray. As I came back to the building, I saw a UPS truck parked out front. Before I had formed a complete thought, my foot was on the back bumper and I was prepared to climb in and hide until the driver took me away.

Common sense prevailed, but my façade crumbled. I stumbled into the main lodge crying hard for the first time during my stay. I was nearing panic when one of the therapists put her arms around me and said, "This is great, Sandy. We've been waiting a long time to see you with snot and mascara all over your face." She found Don, and he reassured me again that situations rarely turn out as awful as we imagine. He had been in sessions with my parents all week and told me that they genuinely wanted reconciliation and healing. Taking a deep, shaky breath, I went to my room, repaired my makeup and prepared for the most difficult afternoon I could conceive.

To Mom with Truth in Love

I began with Mom. Since time began, I am sure that the relationship between mothers and daughters has to have been one of the most complex. Two tenderhearted, emotional beings bound together for a lifetime by their heritage, their sameness and the desire to be cherished by the person who has been the pattern one for the other. For a parent, as I had begun to see with my own children, it is a hope and prayer that we can protect our daughters from venturing down the wrong path, feeling the same hurts and making the same poor choices we had.

Mothers also understand daughters in a way fathers never could, for the same reasons that men don't ask for directions or really want to find their way to full knowledge of the female mind. They've never had a period, budding breasts or worn panty hose, and though they may try, they cannot truly empathize with those who have.

I was fully aware of how volatile my bared emotions could become when I shared with Mom my truth in love list. I was asked to list things that I've never said but should have, and things I had said that were truthful but had been said in the wrong way or at the wrong time. Also to be expressed were things that I felt, needed and expected within the context of the mother-daughter relationship.

For instance, as a child and teenager, I didn't know how to tell Mom that I felt alone and had no one who would listen to me. I was frustrated by her lack of understanding. Because I couldn't express my feelings, I lashed out in anger, saying, "I hate you" and "You don't care about me." I wanted to be able to air these feelings now without becoming angry or hateful. I loved my mom and I wanted to say it and feel it without reservation.

Understanding Mom

I was aware that Mom was nervous, too. Even in my emotional self-absorption I could understand how difficult and frightening this must be for her. I knew, even with little knowledge of psychology, that often the mother is a target for blame when her children have problems. She was there in spite of the knowledge that liability for my eating disorder might end up in her lap.

As I looked at Mom, I thought about what she was like. Her childhood had been difficult, too. The oldest of five children, she was pressed into adult service as caretaker and housekeeper during several of my grandmother's extended illnesses. Her family was far from wealthy, and they moved often. She and her siblings had few luxuries, and even longed for some necessities.

Knowing about her background made me admire her generosity. Mom often gave at the expense of herself. She has always had great compassion for those in need, and gives out of the sheer pleasure of blessing others. When I was a teenager, a Native American missionary came to our church to talk about his work on a reservation out West. He stayed with my family, and remarked many times how beautiful our home was and how he wished his wife could have been there to see it and to meet us. It became clear that his family was poor, and even small luxuries were out of their financial reach.

The day before he left, Mom asked me for a small suitcase that I used for trips to my grandparents. I followed her to her room and watched as she filled it with lotions, powder, scented candles, pantyhose, scarves and other small and pretty things that would warm any woman's heart. As she carefully packed everything in the suitcase, I asked her who all of the goodies were for. She said that if the missionary's wife couldn't come to us, we would send her a few things to brighten her life. I was touched and proud that my mom was so thoughtful. While I understood that my suitcase wouldn't be coming back, I was happy to be part of such a loving gesture.

Waiting for our session to start, I realized that by coming here, Mom was again displaying her generosity of spirit. She often gave plentifully and sacrificially, and now I was the recipient of her abundant heart.

Replaying childhood scenes

We were asked to sit on two sofas, facing each other in a room where my fellow patients and their families would be the audience. They were there for me to support me and observe our exchange. On this stage I would replay the scenes of my life that had injured my soul. Knowing that I would be able later to discuss whatever occurred with someone else was a great help to me. A counselor was behind me on the sofa and another behind Mom, ready to give counsel or to assist in mediation should it become necessary.

I gazed into the eyes of my mother, and saw her nervousness and caution. Although I was hurting, the first words I said to her were, "I love you, and I appreciate your honesty today." I explained that my coldness toward her for the past several years was the result of my fear of exploding with disproportional anger that had stirred in my heart as a result of feeling I could never live up to her expectations.

She responded by saying that she wanted to be there for me in my time of need. Ironically, that triggered my anger again. I wanted to scream out that what she offered was too little and too late. Where was she when I was hurting as a child and a teenager? I needed her now, but I had needed her then, too.

I related the story of the rape to Mom, and cried anew at the memory of my aloneness that stemmed from her disbelief and assumption that I had "asked for it" or just gotten in trouble. It was just one instance in my life when I was made to feel like a bad girl. "Shame on you's" accompanied by looks of disgust played in my head as the prominent features of too many moments in my past.

I explained that I sensed she was ashamed of me in social and family situations where I was less than she wanted me to be. In addition, I also felt her shame as she apologized to others before whom she was embarrassed by my behavior. I could picture the stance and tone of voice that communicated to me that I was in the wrong. I remembered the feeling of knowing that hugs and loving communication would be withheld for a time because I had been bad. I told Mom how, as a child, I had no doubt that she did not love me at those times, and that I felt I had to re-earn her love anew after each infraction.

Mom was patient and, I sensed, quite uncomfortable, listening to my heart and acknowledging my emotions. She stated that Yes, she was often angry with me, for I was a difficult child. She never intended, however, for me to interpret her discipline as a statement that she thought I was bad or that she had not always loved me.

The counselor encouraged us to discuss another issue I had deeply repressed: the molestation by two different family members when I was in my preteen years. It was the hardest thing I had yet done, expressing to Mom the things that members of our family had done to me as a child. Pale but composed, she stated she wanted to believe I was lying, but that she did in fact believe that what I was telling her was true.

This was a new place for me to be with my mom, telling her something awful and hearing her at last verbalizing that she believed me. My inner child mended a bit just by this simple statement. She apologized for what had been done to me by others. I explained that I did not blame her, but I was hurt that I could not come to her for help. I had needed her, but by past experience felt I could not approach her with my story.

At this point Mom and I began to discuss a bit the kind of child I had been. Mom and Pop were strict disciplinarians, and I was a clown and an actress, very adept at manipulating situations until I obtained what I wanted or felt I needed. As I grew into my teen years, deception and lies became part of my repertoire for creating the world I thought I wanted. By sneaking, covering up and shifting blame, I was able to control my circumstances—most of the time. Mom and Pop occasionally caught me in the midst of my schemes, and when they did, a nasty scene ensued, usually resulting in many hurtful words and, on several occasions, physical punishment. I knew that my past behavior had hurt my mom, and for this I apologized. One more instance of mending, this time for Mom.

As I grew into an adult, it seemed that she began to mother me differently. Able to at least pretend to discuss things like rational adults, the manipulation was more obvious and more mutual. I felt pressured to call, to visit and to express my love. I felt that Mom wanted me to assist her with all the things in her life that were messy. Her family relationships, home and health were all burdens I felt she was stacking upon me.

From her, I wanted constant affirmation that I was a good person, mother and wife. I called her when I was depressed or angry, expecting her to make me feel better. It seemed that we could not talk on the phone without leaving the discussion with the feeling that we each had a job to do for the other, and if it wasn't accomplished, "we ought to be ashamed of ourselves." Ironically, we both often were.

Too much sweetness?

My present relationship with Mom and my two small girls became the root of our final discussion from my truth in love list. It seemed to me that Mom was smothering my girls with love and affection and "stuff" to somehow appease her own guilt over our past stormy relationship. I was angry for the way I perceived I had been treated as a child, and I resented her closeness with my girls.

A part of me felt that somehow Mom was trying to get me to see that she really was a good parent—just look how wonderful she was to my children. It hurt to see her work at her relationship with them in a way I had never seen her work at loving me. Her sweetness toward them overwhelmed me; it was like eating too much sugar. I wanted to remind her that I knew who she really was and was not fooled. The comedian Bill Cosby has said that grandparents are parents who are trying to get into heaven. That hit a little too close to home for me to find it funny.

Although I knew I was being disproportionate, and in great part unfair, these emotions had to be laid on the table and talked through, for they were one last hurdle to complete openness. Mom expressed that she supposed in part she was overdoing things with my girls, but it was her chance to do what constraints of both time and finances had never allowed her to do when her own children were young.

We caught our breath and rested from our discussion, and I felt as though a great weight had begun to lift. Like dumping out a trash bag, everything had been looked through, and we were all still there, sitting in the same room staring at it. No one had thrown anything or lost control. And, most importantly, no one had walked away.

The counselor encouraged us to discuss what we wanted for the future of our relationship. I looked at my list and began to read these "I needs" and "I expects":

- I need honesty between us.
- I need you to own your feelings and take care of yourself.
- I need you to follow your own advice.
- I need grown-up mother-love and support, not smothering.
- I need for you not to pressure me to visit and call; I have my own family now.
- I expect you to let me grow up.
- I expect a good relationship to begin here.
- I expect you to understand that my healing and recovery will be a process.

First step on a journey

I'd like to say that there were hugs and tears all around, and that every bad feeling went away in that moment, but it was not so. My healing process with my mom had just begun. Family Week was the first lesson of many on how to walk through past hurts in this all-powerful relationship. I saw Mom's hurts, too, and her pain. Although I was still suspicious of her motives in some areas, I could see her sincere and loving effort to be honest and aware in a new way. She accepted who I was, why I had come to this point and how I needed her to mother me in the future in order to assist in my recovery.

In retrospect, it is clear to me that it took great courage for my mom to come to Family Week. Our society often blames the mother when a daughter has emotional problems, and here I was asking her to walk into an unknown situation in a psychiatric hospital where I was being treated. With no idea how she would be received, she willingly came and allowed herself to become part of my treatment process.

Because of her love and desire to help me, we now have the relationship I have always wanted. We are honest with one another and discuss subjects that used to be forbidden territory. We are friends, and I am deeply grateful to have a mother who has stood with me as I put my life back together.

Encounter with Pop

After a short break, we moved back to the same sofas to begin again. This time, my discussion would be with Pop, my stepfather. As an adult, I felt that my relationship with him was damaged and very incomplete.

From Daddy to Pop

My heart had always ached over the loss of Daddy, my first father, and Pop had made it clear that he was uncomfortable stepping into shoes he could never hope to fill. Wanting me to call him by his first name out of respect for my father put a distance between us. I would not understand until many years later that this established line would leave me always yearning for more from him. I was the one who settled on "Pop." It was very important to me, for it was as close as I could get to making him my dad.

In many ways, I strove to make Pop love me in a way that would someday cause him to say, "Please, Sandy, call me Daddy." In those same moments, I was also toying with an idealistic vision of how my real daddy would have been different, would have never punished, spanked or become impatient.

I missed my daddy desperately after he died. From the time Mom began dating Pop, I wanted him to be my new daddy and love me and let me love him in return. I didn't discover until many years later the many reasons why he could not open his heart completely to me. I was just a little girl who wanted to be loved. I was also energetic, inquisitive, loud, careless and irresponsible. My need for attention caused me to seek it in ways that got me in trouble, but I discovered that even negative attention was better than none at all. I soon found out that while he could be great fun, Pop also had a temper that flared quickly. I was the catalyst for that anger most of the time, and while I didn't always understand why I was in trouble, there was no question that he was angry with me.

Life with Pop

Pop is known as a hard worker. He works hard to keep his home in tiptop condition, and he works equally hard for others. His handprints are all over the church where I grew up. He painted the interior and exterior, revamped and improved the sound system and pitched in on more men's breakfasts than I can count.

As a child, I remember his coming home from a long day of painting for a living, then going right to work on the house or the yard. Some of it was maintenance and some was improvement. He made it a comfortable and beautiful home. He and Mom bought a neglected and unfinished house soon after they married. He put sweat equity into it, making it a place we were all proud of.

The other side of Pop's hard work was extreme perfectionism. He expected a lot from himself and from his family. My personality was on the other end of the scale. I was sloppy and inattentive to detail. My inability or lack of desire to do things Pop's way triggered many of our clashes. When he became angry because I didn't go along with his program, I internalized it and believed that he just didn't like me. I felt unworthy of his affection because I couldn't live up to his standards.

When we fought, it affected the entire family. Debbie would go to her room to escape the shouting, and Mom tried to referee. The older I got, the worse it became. It seemed that I somehow realized I was going to be in trouble no matter what, so I went to extremes with my behavior. Don summed it up nicely in one therapy session. He said, "You figured you were going to get in trouble no matter what you did, so you decided that you might as well blow it out your shorts." It was a very apt description because the older I got, the more extreme my provocative behavior became.

Along with times of strife, my childhood is scattered with memories of happy times with Pop. We packed the camper and went to state parks. He took Debbie and me hiking or swimming, allowing Mom to relax with a book. I especially loved fishing with him. We would take sandwiches and fish for hours, catching bluegill, throwing them back and catching them again. When my seventh-grade teacher nicknamed me "Sam," Pop used it too, saying that it fit my tomboyish personality. I tried very hard to be good and do things right, hoping that the feeling of contentment and companionship of these times with Pop would last.

Fear, anger and love

Now, as I looked across the short space toward Pop, I felt an unreasonable fear rising in my heart. Would he reject me, scold me or distance himself right here in front of this audience? I didn't want them to see how unworthy I was of his love.

Facing him on that couch during Family Week, I was torn. Part of me wanted to climb into his lap and beg him to love me, and part of me wanted to rip his head off for terrorizing me with his anger during my childhood.

The "truth in love" list asked me to express first some "I feels." More than anything, I felt angry because I had been raised in an angry home, where Pop's moods dictated the pace of daily living. I have found that this is common among his generation. Men were taught very little about restraining their emotions, or for that matter even acknowledging them. Strong men had strong passions, felt strongly about things and were bound to let off steam and lose their tempers.

But my years of yearning for approval, coupled with Pop's tendency to present himself forcefully, had left me mad, resentful and feeling that I was a failure in his eyes—a screw-up who could never amount to much. I imagined him happy to see me leave home when I moved out on my own. I imagined myself also happy with this, but in my little girl's heart, I left with an aching need for approval, which would take me searching for father-love from the wrong guys in the wrong way for years to come.

From Pop's point of view

As I expressed to Pop my fear and resentment, he faced me head-on. He admitted that he had punished in anger when I was young, that he had yelled at me as a form of discipline very often because he was afraid of what his temper might release on me if he did anything more physical. I was the child who rubbed his nerves in the wrong direction. If the truth were told, I suspect I knew that; but at least he gave me lots of attention in those moments. He certainly couldn't ignore me. I remember seeing a comic strip in which a dad is looking at a child as he states, "I have one nerve left, and you're on it." It made me cry to think of it, for it encapsulated the vicious cycle of my relationship with Pop.

The verbal discipline Pop dispensed included many words of harsh criticism. More than anything else, this left its stamp on me. I could remember the essence of those words, the underlying message, regardless of what was actually said. My interpretation was that he felt I would never amount to anything. I was selfish, incompetent, lazy, foolish, unworthy of his time and a person with whom he would just never be able to see eye to eye. In other words, someone he would avoid contact with until it was absolutely required.

Pop began to open up his heart at this point, explaining that he fell in love with my mom, and that love was a package deal. When he married Mom, he knew he was accepting responsibility for her children as well. He explained that in those first years, he was under constant pressure from his ex-wife, responsibility for his two children from that marriage and his desire to make a home for his new family. He admitted that his first thought was to be a good provider for my sister and me, but that as time went on he grew to love us as well.

In that moment, sitting across from Pop, I realized that this was new territory for him, and I asked him to consider another of the "I needs" listed on my truth in love list. I told him I needed to hear his emotions. I needed for him to voice them to me so that I would understand how he felt inside—not the explosion of anger, but the root cause of that anger or hurt. Pop had always given pronouncements of his views, but was not adept at elaboration. I watched him carefully as he began to tell me of his childhood, his father.

Pop explained that he could not remember ever being hugged by his father. The adage that "Children are to be seen, not heard" was the rule in his childhood. His father saw him from time to time, but that was probably all. Pop had never been taught how to father, for he had never really been fathered himself. In turn, Pop's father hadn't been taught how to fulfill that role. It struck me anew how truly overwhelming the impact of our experiences can be on generations to come.

I told him how angry I was that he had spanked and disciplined me so harshly that I was afraid of him. He countered with his feelings of frustration that I had been so "hard headed" and just wouldn't listen. Describing how badly he felt after one especially severe spanking, he said he had vowed never to hit me again. He was afraid of hurting me in his anger, but he was frustrated because he didn't know how to control me.

Suddenly Pop pounded the wall behind the couch where we sat, demonstrating the frustration he'd felt during my teen years. My response was immediate and visceral. I jumped backward into the lap of the therapist sitting behind me and started to cry.

Looking kindly at me, Pop extended an olive branch, saying, "I'd like to try again, to go fishing, fly a kite." He told me that he needed to know what I expected of him as a father and as a person. He expressed that he would like to have a relationship with me that was independent of Mom. We had never had that. Because of all our conflict, Mom had always been the mediator of most of our communication. As adults we had learned to discuss safe things—the kids, the weather, Scott's career and, to a small degree, things involving faith, politics and economics.

It was not easy for him to speak of these things; I could see by his body language that he was uncomfortable. But he was trying; he was there and he was trying.

Mixed Emotions

Often confused by conflicting emotions I was just beginning to understand, I experienced a mixture of anger and softness as I listened to Pop give voice to his emotions.

First I was angry. All of the other families really liked Pop. He's funny, he had encouraged other family members and once he had saved the day by fixing the coffeemaker when it quit working. While I knew that the other patients and their families could see the love and concern on Pop's face, I was remembering the times I had seen rage or disappointment there.

I also felt my heart beginning to soften toward this man who had so obviously stepped out of his comfort zone to come and support Mom and to help me toward wellness.

In closing, he implored me to get well. He encouraged me to do whatever I had to do, and promised that he would help in every way he was capable. He was reaching, and he didn't have to. I began to feel that I wasn't alone.

However, I had an unreasonable fear that if I left this place arm-in-arm with my family (at sunset of course) I would be expected to live happily ever after with all of them. I still needed some affirmation that I had had a tough childhood, and some recognition of how difficult it would be to create a new relationship from the ashes of one that had not been good for any of us.

It seemed that there was still a lot of work to do. I feared I was not strong enough. I had failed everyone so miserably for so many years, especially my stepfather. How would it ever be possible to create a new relationship based on love and trust?

I had lived in a hell of my own creation through my struggle with bulimia. My family was beginning to understand that it had not been the result of one bad decision or one bad habit, but was instead the culmination of many years of hurts, wants and corrupted images. No one was specifically to blame, but we each had work to do to repair the breaches of trust and to build on the love we had just expressed to one another.

Mom and Pop couldn't save me, couldn't rewind my childhood, but they were at last able to understand better why I was who I was. They still loved me, and I think that in that moment they loved me more for all my own openness and need. Yet, although they would be there for me in the future, I knew that the toughest discussion was to come. I still needed to share the truth in love with the person who meant more to me than anyone in the world: my husband, Scott.

Love Means Never Having to Say You're Sorry, and Other Lies

Love bears all things, believes all things, hopes all things, and endures all things. Love never fails.

—1 Corinthians 13:7-8 (NASB)

Other than salvation through Christ, my husband Scott is the best thing that ever happened to me. In the midst of my self-destructive behavior and miserable existence, God placed a man who would walk beside me throughout my healing.

I was more than terrified at the thought of facing Scott as part of my Family Week therapy. My relationship with him was by far the most powerful in my life. In my mind, he was the perfect husband, and I wanted desperately to be his perfect wife. I felt vulnerable to hurts that I feared would come as he expressed himself, and I was ashamed that I had let my Prince Charming down so badly.

People are drawn to Scott. He's somewhat private, but also intelligent and funny, and he's easy to talk to. The first thing you notice about him are his deep-green, piercing eyes. They can be full of fun or steely, and his gaze holds you as he speaks. His personality also shows itself in the way he carries himself. Scott doesn't just walk—he strides. His footsteps eat up the ground, shoulders squared, head high. He's a man on a mission. Imagine all of that in a fighter pilot's flight suit and boots coming toward me across the tarmac and you'll understand why my heart did flip-flops the first time I saw him.

Knight in Shining Flight Suit

When we met and began to date, I was overwhelmed by Scott's genuine interest in me. He liked my sense of humor, the way I handled my job and he loved the fact that I didn't mind getting my hair messed up when we rode in his car with the top down. We liked the same music, loved airplanes and he even tolerated my poorly trained dog. We took long walks at twilight, picked berries and went out to eat. He met me at the Officer's Club after work and I was secure in his presence. It wasn't long before I began to see him as my knight in shining armor. In his case, it was a green flight suit, and his horse was an ugly jet; but he was my rescuer. I felt good about myself when I was with him. At first we were both dating other people, but before long we were seeing each other exclusively. I wanted him all to myself because in him I saw a way out of the mess I called my life.

With Scott, I didn't have to drink to feel witty and relaxed. Assured that he loved me, I wasn't attracted to other men. The pain and insecurities that had haunted me seemed farther away. I was almost literally "high." It seemed I had found someone to fix me and make my life all better.

We had been dating for about six months when I got orders to leave England and report to an Air Force base in

Arizona. I didn't want to go. Leaving Scott was unthinkable, but once the orders were issued, I was locked into them. There was only one way I could stay in England. If we got married, the military would extend my stay until the end of his tour.

My first marriage had been a disaster because I united with my ex-husband out of a longing to be loved and taken care of. He had turned out to be an abusive budding alcoholic. I had been divorced three years, and didn't want to have to go through that again. I wondered if my marriage with Scott would last because my motives for marrying him were very much the same as the first time. I didn't know, but my dread of being alone outweighed the fear of making another mistake.

Scott asked me to marry him, and the ceremony took place less than a year after we met. Traveling to the States for the wedding, we started getting acquainted with each other's families, and then returned to England. Our first home was a farm cottage in the English countryside. It was quaint and pretty, with paned windows, no heat except a coal stove in the kitchen, and green fields all around. Our only close neighbors were chickens. Even the house's name was romantic. It was called "Vale Cottage," and had a rose garden in front and primroses along the gravel driveway.

With two salaries, we were able to travel. We had some great times seeing Europe. Our honeymoon was a backpacking trip through Greece. Six months after we married we flew to Athens with rented gear and a sense of adventure. Staying in out-of-the-way places, we saw Greece from a peasant's perspective. I was sure that life couldn't possibly be more idyllic as we drove a rented Jeep around the island of Naxos, stopping for lunch at the hovel of one of the natives. The sun was hot and the air smelled of the oregano, thyme and jasmine that grew wild. We toured museums, ate fresh seafood and fruit. I had a most memorable argument with a taxi driver who spoke no English. Life was wonderful, because I was with the man I loved. He loved me, and I had assured his continuing love by losing 30 pounds.

Looking back, it seems silly to equate outer appearance with inner peace. At the time, it made perfect sense. With a loving husband and lots of compliments to boost my self-esteem, I thought that being thin and married was the key to a happy life. At that point I had no clue that my past pain would interfere with my ability to have a healthy relationship.

As all married couples do, we found that living together uncovered each other's irritating little habits and personality quirks. Scott wanted certain things done his way, and if I let the stove go out or forgot to close the garage door, he became very irritated. He was finding out that I wasn't flawless, and I discovered that he wasn't either. Quite honestly, though, I assumed that his imperfections were somehow my fault. If I could get my act together and be the wife he deserved, he wouldn't ever be angry or picky about small things.

I had a legitimate longing to be cherished and protected and safe. As a child, a father didn't fulfill those longings. Unconsciously, I looked to Scott to fill these longings, not just to be my husband but also a father figure. He didn't know what I expected of him; and, to be honest, neither did I. There was just emptiness in my heart that ached to be filled. That empty place was meant to be filled with a father's love. It would be a long time before I learned that not just any man could provide the nurturing love that was missing. Scott walked into a relationship that demanded more than he could be expected to give. Needs, longings and wounds from my past would create chaos in our marriage.

The Conflict Gap

Scott's family is very pragmatic. They deal with problems and conflict very efficiently, and feelings rarely enter the solution. His parents are intelligent, loving people who desire the best for their children. Scott's childhood was free from trauma. Life with his parents and sister revolved around extended family, routine and play. An Eagle Scout, Scott and his father were actively involved in Boy Scouts. His mother contributed love and warmth to her family. She cooked from scratch, sewed and gave her children a rich heritage of special traditions and memories.

Family trips were a big part of every summer. They saw much of the United States in their travels. Honesty, hard work and responsibility were stressed. Because of this, Scott grew into a confident, intelligent and analytical man. While he is very loving, expressing feelings has never come easily for him.

I had never been taught how to resolve conflicts. My solution was rebellion, shouting and throwing a tantrum. As a result, Scott and I handled conflict very differently. A perfect example occurred after a storm had knocked out electricity at our cottage. The pump for the well had to be re-primed, requiring a trip down a trapdoor in the lawn to the wellhead. Scott carried a kettle of water, and climbed through the trapdoor. My task was to reset the electrical breaker, then run upstairs and flush the toilet, which would create suction to get water flowing into the system again.

Unfortunately, I didn't hear him yell "flush," so I was shocked when I stuck my head out the window and he asked me in a rather nasty tone if I was deaf. My heart twisted and I reacted without thought. First I screamed an obscenity at him, then ran down to the kitchen, pulled a pitcher of water out of the refrigerator, stomped outside and poured the water on his head as he looked up from the wellhead in shock. Then I ran and hid—first in the barn, then in a bean field—for four hours.

I was afraid he would be furious with me and I couldn't face it. When I finally went home, he laughed. Rather than being angry, he was tickled by my spunk. His only concern was the nasty language I used. "Why do you have to yell and curse?" he asked. The fact was that I didn't know any other way to fight.

At an early age, I had decided to be very careful not to marry a man like my stepfather. His temper scared me and his perfectionism made him impossible to please. Growing up with anger and criticism was bad enough. I wasn't about to spend my adult life dealing with the same things. Any time Scott was aggravated with me, I became frightened. His behavior may have been normal and not unkind, but in my mind I was transported to my childhood when I couldn't do anything right. When Scott questioned how I did something or suggested a better way, it sounded critical. Echoes of fear edged into my heart like ripples in a pond. I was an adult, but my responses to conflict were those of a child.

Voices from the Child Within

Imagine an adult woman walking through life with a three-year-old child who is telling her how to react and what to feel in every situation. When Scott had to be away from home for a few days or a few weeks, my three-year-old self told me that I was being abandoned. It seemed just like my daddy going away. I was afraid Scott wouldn't come back. Traveling is a fact of military life, but I was angry and resented him for leaving. The entire emotional process went on without my conscious input. I couldn't connect my adult feelings of anger with my childhood memories of abandonment. I just felt mad and unreasonably frightened.

Once, when Scott was working in Germany for three weeks and I was at home in England, he called me to say that he missed me and to see how I was doing. I took his absence personally and was angry with him. Expecting him to know how I felt, I waited for him to apologize. Instead, I listened as he described the weekend ski trip he had taken with his buddies. After a very frustrating conversation, I hung up without saying good-bye, then picked up the telephone and threw it as hard as I could on the floor. It broke into several pieces. There wasn't enough left to answer even if I wanted to. What was wrong with me? Why did I act that way? I broke the phone in rage, but also to punish Scott so that he couldn't call me back after I hung up on him.

My insecurity showed in other areas, too. In the car after doing errands one Saturday, Scott made a few comments and suggestions about my driving. Rather than evaluating his remarks and choosing to accept or decline his help, I slammed on the brakes and got out of the car, screaming at him, "If you don't like my driving, then *you* drive. I'm walking the 10 miles home." He ended up driving slowly beside me as I walked along the roadside, apologizing until I relented and got back in the car.

Any remark that I construed as criticism set me off. In my mind, criticism and love could not coexist. If Scott didn't like my actions, then he didn't love me. The little Sandy inside me was still reacting to being scolded harshly for minor offenses.

For nine years of our marriage, Scott walked on eggshells around me while I heard reproach in everything he said, saw it in every look. He is highly disciplined and a perfectionist, and I automatically transferred my feelings concerning my stepfather to him. I didn't fight fair. I learned to resolve conflict by shouting, crying and sometimes hitting. It was the only way I knew how to fight, and it made our marriage tense and unhappy. Rather than solving the natural problems that arise in any relationship, we either fought or ignored them and hoped they would go away.

The biggest barrier to a better relationship with Scott was my lack of understanding. I didn't know that I was seeing someone else in his actions. Looking back, it is clear that I subconsciously expected Scott to treat me like the men who had wounded me sexually, physically and emotionally. I didn't trust him not to hurt me. Even in God I saw characteristics of men who had abused me. I assumed that Scott and God were just waiting for me to mess up so they could hammer me.

It is normal for babies or toddlers to assume that the whole world revolves around them. They see people and feelings as an extension of themselves. Normally, as children grow and mature, they begin to view themselves as separate from others. I was in my 30s before I realized that I was not a part of every feeling other people displayed before me. Physically grown up, I lived as an adult and spoke with an adult voice, but emotionally I was still a child. My reactions were childish and I reasoned as a child.

On Valentine's Day the year before I sought help for my eating disorder, Scott sent me a dozen red roses. He was leaving the next day for a month of training in another state, and I was trying to do all of my errands before he left. I wanted to go to the grocery store without the girls, and Scott was reluctant to let me go. We argued, and I accused him of trying to control everything I did. As I cried, the doorbell rang and Scott asked me to answer it. I refused, because my eyes were red from crying.

Finally, he went to the door and came back with a large, white box. He laid it gently on my lap and told me that he had wanted me to stay home so I would be surprised by the delivery of flowers. I took the lid off of the box, saw and smelled the roses and threw them at him. "I don't deserve roses," I screamed. "I'm nasty and I don't know how you can stand me." I felt truly awful.

In treatment, a counselor asked me about my marriage. I told him that it wasn't good, but that my husband was great, in fact perfect. All of our problems were my fault. He looked at me and asked, "If Scott is so perfect, why did he marry *you*?" That surprised me, and made me think. It was the beginning of comprehending that when a relationship is dysfunctional, both people have some work to do. Until that point, I had saddled Scott with being perfect. Since I believed him to be perfect, I was extremely upset when he showed signs of being human. Part of the reason he had to walk on eggshells around me was that I didn't feel safe when he made mistakes. I was so terribly insecure in myself, I depended totally on him for safety.

I operated chiefly out of my heart, Scott out of his head. Consequently, my feelings got in the way when we had a problem or conflict. Because Scott is so analytical, he rarely connected feelings to what he saw as a logical problem-solving process. In contrast, my feelings were so intense I couldn't put them aside to look at a problem rationally.

In short, I was afraid of Family Week with Scott because for the first time I understood the extent of our differences. How would we approach each other?

Scott and Family Week

Scott was walking into the middle of my treatment very unprepared. I had shared some of my new insights with him over the phone and in letters, but all of it was newer to him than it was to me. He heard me say things such as "I'm not crazy like I thought I was. I'm just sick," and "My reactions to you have been all wrong. I'm learning how to be strong." At that time, he had no experience to help him understand what I was saying. It was as though I was learning to speak a new language that he knew nothing about.

Fear of telling all

As I've said, "truth in love" is the focus of Family Week. Addictions, including eating disorders, flourish in secrecy. Once the truth is out in the open, everyone involved can deal with it, and with the pain involved. Telling Scott all of my secrets made Family Week ghastly for me. I had not only hidden years of bingeing, purging and secret drinking from him, I never told him about my shameful past. Now I could no longer avoid the issues. No more lies. I had to come clean about everything of which I was most ashamed.

An excerpt from my journal during that week clearly states how I felt:

> *Scott's here for Family Week. I am pretty scared about him coming, and how he will react to the changes in me. He seems positive, likes seeing me smiling and optimistic. My goal for this week is to bravely show him who I really am and stop being codependent. He says he doesn't feel like he needs to examine any feelings or change anything about himself, and I don't like being the one who has to do all of the improving.*

Learning that accepting and expressing feelings was essential to mental health made it even scarier to face Scott. I desperately wanted to be able to communicate with him, but I didn't know if we could find common ground. I thought if I tried to be more analytical and he was more emotional, we would finally be able to understand each other. The most frightening possibility that I could imagine was that he might refuse to be part of the change, and we could never have the relationship I longed for.

Sitting across from the man I loved on that couch, I wondered if he would still love me when all of my secrets were out. He would get to talk first. I knew by then I could choose how to react to the things he had to say. Still, I feared I would crumble if he became angry or disappointed.

From fear to security

Hearing Scott express feelings startled me. He was more vulnerable than I had ever seen him. Using words like scared, worried, cheated and angry, he told me how my emotional illness affected him.

A part of me recoiled at hearing him say that he hated knowing that I kept so many secrets from him. He was angry because I lied about my eating disorder. After nine years of marriage, he wondered if he really knew me at all. I was too shocked even to cry as he told me how afraid he was that I might die. My heart melted when he said that I was his best friend and he didn't want to lose me. Seeing tears in his eyes convinced me that he truly loved me. For the first time, I felt secure in his commitment to me.

I told him truthfully about all of my lies and deception. My secret life had been so difficult to maintain that I was relieved to finally admit it. I was terribly afraid of rejection, but I came completely clean. He was clearly shocked to hear the details of my drinking and bulimia. Asking for forgiveness was frightening. What if he couldn't forgive me? How could I survive if he was so disgusted by my behavior that he didn't love me anymore? And I wasn't done yet. The hidden alcohol and furtive vomiting were bad enough. Now I had to tell him about the sexual abuse, beatings and promiscuity.

Scott was stunned to learn the secrets from my past. He said that he wished he had known more about my disease and the loneliness I had felt. But instead of being repulsed by my history, he was glad we were getting to the root of my problems, and he looked forward to working on our relationship.

One evening during that week we sat in a swing on the lawn and talked about what we had discovered about one another. Both of us were relieved that the worst was over and the healing could begin. I was comforted by his anger at those who had hurt me, and he was glad to hear me say that I wanted complete honesty in our relationship in the future.

Family Week answered a lot of Scott's questions. Learning about my past enabled him to understand why I was so emotionally fragile. I had not felt unconditionally loved, and I expected to be rejected by men. Because of my experiences and the way I had learned to cope with them, I hadn't been able to believe that Scott truly loved me and wouldn't leave me. His inability to empathize and express feelings only made me feel worse. Now I knew it was because he didn't know how, not because he didn't want to.

Turning down the heat

During that week, Scott drew a picture that perfectly illustrated our marriage. It showed him in a pot of boiling water with a fire blazing underneath. He was leaning over the side of the pot adding wood to the fire with one hand, and using a fire extinguisher trying to put it out with the other. He explained that I was the pot of water, and the fire symbolized wounds from my past. He hadn't started the fire that was making life with me unbearable, but he was feeding the blaze without meaning to. Not comprehending my wounds and insecurities, he fed them with insensitivity and ignorance of my illness.

The fire began to die during Family Week. I was putting my past in order, and Scott was learning ways of communicating that didn't add fuel to the dying blaze. The temperature of the water became much more comfortable, but it was still hot. Knowing the problem and understanding its roots are only the beginning of the solution. Learning ways of getting along and breaking old habits takes time and practice.

By the end of Family Week, it was clear that my marriage was turning a corner. We both knew there was still work to be done. Scott went home to work and care for our children.

As for me, my assignments were independence, autonomy, honesty and assertiveness. I buckled down to practice what I was learning and to become more secure in my recovery.

Learning to Fly

But those who hope in the* L*ORD* *will renew their strength. They will soar on wings like eagles.

—Isaiah 40:31

I spent the remainder of my time in treatment accomplishing several tasks. I needed more practice recognizing and expressing emotions. Identifying feelings and situations at home that could trigger the "urge to purge" was crucial. Listing the ways I could counter the desire to return to my eating disorder gave me confidence that I would not slip back into a destructive pattern of dealing with stress by abusing food. I spent many hours reflecting on my past and trying to understand how it affected my life in the present.

Confidence became a wonderfully familiar feeling. Not as worried about my appearance and actions, I loosened up and had fun. I felt strong enough to mentor new patients as they came in. I rode, swam (comfortable in a bathing suit!), worked hard in therapy, practiced making food choices and made exploratory visits to restaurants.

Signs of Deliverance

The most unexpected experience at this point was the realization that many of those on staff were people I would choose as friends. I was seeing myself as a person who was growing, rather than as a victim or sick person. Talking to the nurses, mental health technicians, doctors, dietitians and therapists, I recognized they also had imperfect lives. Yet they were healthy because they recognized their problems and confronted them. When I mentioned this to Don, he said, "It's a sign you're ready for discharge when you start seeing yourself as an equal with the staff."

Elated and nervous, I began to make preparations to leave. The Ranch felt like a part of me, but I yearned to return to my family. Knowing I still had a long way to go, I nevertheless felt strong enough to switch to outpatient care.

My last day finally arrived. After three months in treatment, it was time to go home. I felt ready to fly. In the space of 72 days, my perceptions of life and myself had been radically altered. I recognized and embraced reality. My prison of perfection was crumbling. Like someone liberated from years within real prison walls, I was excited by everything the world had to offer, but intimidated by the choices I had to make.

A different Sandy stood at the airport in Phoenix, waiting to board the plane. My carry-on bag was bulging with simple gifts from people who cared about me. Lemons from a backyard tree, a copy of the video *The Princess Bride* to remind me to laugh, a small clay cactus—mementos of the Southwest. Brown ooze no longer shamed or tormented me. My fingernails were short and clean, utilitarian, and that was OK with me. Out of the wasteland of my life, God had begun a wondrous thing. Reality—He was teaching me to deal with reality. What a concept. Rather than deny the pain of the present or run from my past, I wanted to experience life and all of its feelings.

A living, breathing example of God's grace, I felt ready to rejoin my family.

During my time away, I had been too busy and daunted by my tasks in therapy to feel homesick very often. Now, waves of longing for my children and husband washed over me as I looked out of a window in the airplane that was speeding me home.

Homecoming

At the airport, Scott, Anne and Lauren waited for me. As I walked across the ramp to the entrance to the terminal, I could see two little girls dancing with anticipation by the window as they watched me approach. I felt overwhelmed with love as I dropped my bags and fell to my knees to receive their embraces. After the initial round of hugs, Lauren stepped back and studied me intently. I returned her gaze, realizing that she was reconciling me with the memory she had of her mom. Understanding that it was indeed Mommy, she rushed at me for another hug. Anne held fast to my hand the whole time, talking and trying to say everything at once.

In the van on the way home, we alternated between talking and asking questions all at once and awkward silences where we didn't know what to say. Driving down the street toward our house I felt a time-warp sensation. I had left Wisconsin in January when the snow was deep. It was April now; the air was damp and fresh, but not cold. Buds were forming on trees and the earliest bulbs pushed green points out of the earth. One season had passed and another had begun while I was gone.

Walking into the house through the garage, I was enveloped in the unique and familiar fragrance of my home. Pleasant odors of dried eucalyptus, potpourri and various cleaning supplies mingled to welcome me. My cat sat at the top of the stairs, ears and tail twitching a hello.

I toured the house, closely followed by the girls who were intent on telling me everything that happened while I was gone. The house looked the same, with subtle changes. The canisters and cookbooks on the kitchen counter had been rearranged. Plants were in different spots. Everything was meticulously clean. I complimented Scott on his housekeeping and felt a twinge of sadness that they had gotten along so well without me! He told me that he had done his best, and that everyone from our parents and friends to people from our church had lent a hand cooking, cleaning and doing laundry.

Hearing about those who had supported my family reminded me that I was in familiar yet uncharted territory. When I left, I had lied to all of my friends about where I was going. While in treatment, I wrote to several of them and told them what was really going on. I was looking forward to seeing everyone and sharing with them all that God was doing to heal my heart, mind and body. A little hesitant about sharing the messier details of my eating disorder and its roots, I was buoyed by the love and acceptance I had received in treatment.

Before I could make plans to visit friends, I had lots of catching up to do with my daughters. The older one, Anne, has always been mature beyond her years, and now she was proud of the new responsibilities she had taken on while I was gone. She showed me her school papers from kindergarten and told me she could make her own lunch now.

Before I left, I had carefully controlled the kitchen and wouldn't allow the girls to get into the refrigerator or prepare any food. Here was one area where I could immediately begin to change, to loosen my compulsive control.

Lauren, the younger daughter, was proud of her ability to choose her own clothes and brush and arrange her hair. Her mismatched outfit and crooked ponytail reminded me that I had an opportunity not to obsess about my children's appearance.

A neighbor's casserole went into the oven to provide my first dinner at home. I was tired and hungry, and didn't stop to analyze the ingredients until I was almost through eating. Comparing what was in it to the food plan I was given upon discharge, I found that while I would not have chosen to make tuna casserole, it still worked nicely into my dietary plan. What a sense of freedom—to eat without guilt.

Back to Everyday Realities

Within a matter of days, I was back into the routine of caring for a family and home. I felt fragile and emotionally exposed, however, and I wished I still had counselors living with me to help me dissect every stress and difficult situation. Scott was home the first week, and then was scheduled to go on a three-day trip. As his trip approached, I became more and more apprehensive.

Treatment had required hard emotional work, but there was the professional staff to help me and the support staff to take care of mundane but necessary trivia such as cooking and cleaning the bathroom. Now it was all up to me. I had to learn how to put together the tasks of staying emotionally and physically healthy while dealing with the details of being a wife and mother—not to mention being an aircraft maintenance officer one weekend a month.

Nervousness descended when the reality of being at home hit me. I was back in the very same situation and circumstances that caused me to binge, purge and starve in the first place. The kids still fought and talked back to me, Scott was still a demanding perfectionist, the house still got dirty and the cat's litter box still smelled. Old ways of coping rose to the surface. It left me feeling shaky when Anne helped herself to a snack and left a mess or Lauren insisted on wearing two different shoes on the wrong feet. Scott's need for clean and pressed shirts for his trip reminded me that I had forgotten to do the laundry.

Like a driver on a raceway skidding out of control, I gripped the wheel, stood on the brakes and tried desperately to maintain control. Old feelings of inferiority and a sense of being overwhelmed suffocated me. I had several options, I realized. I could binge and purge or starve to relieve the fear and pressure, or I could call on my "pit crew" for help. Gathering up my few remaining shreds of control, I asked Scott to cancel his trip and stay home for a few more days. It was hard to ask and appear weak, but asking for what I needed was one of the main things I had learned in therapy.

Using the metaphor of someone who has been hospitalized with pneumonia, I told Scott that I needed more time to get secure on my feet. He has an ironclad work ethic, and I know it was difficult for him, but he agreed. He called his chief pilot and asked for the extra time off.

I was relieved for two reasons. One, I got the help that I needed; and two, I asked for help rather than using an addiction to cope. And it worked. I could admit that I was vulnerable and not feel degraded or weak. Scott's loving validation of my need gave me courage for the next time that I would need to ask for support. I was used to getting my needs met by manipulating—basically pouting or getting mad because Scott "should know" what I wanted or needed.

I used to believe that if he really loved me, he wouldn't have to ask. Now I could see that it was easier for both of us when I didn't play mind games.

Coming Clean with Friends

Now that I was home and settling in, friends called and stopped by. Some were cautious and some direct about asking about my time away and about my eating disorder. Most were surprised and delighted to find a relaxed, funny Sandy in the place of the tightly controlled false smile they had last seen. These people didn't realize yet that before I went into treatment, I wouldn't even answer the door unless I was expecting someone. The thought of letting someone in if the house wasn't in perfect order terrified me.

Before therapy I could never have overcome the shame of my past enough to share my life story with friends. Only a handful of people really knew where I had been and why. As others approached me and asked about my absence, I experimented with what to say and how much to tell. I spent some time before coming home thinking about whom and what I would tell about my past and my eating disorder. I knew that there were those whom I could trust with the whole truth, and others with whom I would need to be more circumspect. I wasn't as much worried that they might tell someone what I had been through as I was nervous about their reaction. I felt fragile, and knew it would be hard to cope if someone invalidated my experiences or rejected me because of my past.

Those who knew me well confided that they had wondered about my health before I left. I was sick quite a lot because the lack of adequate nutrition had compromised my immune system. I was also very thin, but when asked if I was well I would reply that I was "just fine." At that time I assumed that they were jealous because I was the thinnest mom on the block. Now remorseful for lying to people who cared about me, it felt good to "come clean" about my behavior before treatment. With God's help I told acquaintances that I had an eating disorder and had gone away for treatment. Those whom I knew better got more detailed information about the roots of my problem.

I had struggled and had a crisis in treatment with the issue of faith as the key to healing. In my time away I had concluded that God rarely unholsters His powerful right hand and instantaneously heals people. It has happened, and miracles occur daily, but God did not choose to heal me that way. He knew that I would benefit more from the process of getting well than from instant health. My new understanding was that I must continue to work through issues and work on recovery. I would need faith to believe that there was nothing I couldn't do or overcome with God's help and power.

My friend Marlene told me that God showed her Philippians 1:6 and asked her to encourage me with it. It says "Being confident of this, that he who began a good work in you will carry it on to completion until the day of Christ Jesus." I only needed to admit that I was weak and to rely on God's strength one day at a time. Miraculously enough, the urges to purge, binge and avoid eating were gone. When I was stressed, I was afraid it might return, but it wasn't a daily compulsion. Relying on God's strength was what would bring me victory when I felt compelled to use those old coping mechanisms.

Some people in the Christian community seriously questioned my wisdom in going through therapy. They saw psychological help as a departure from Scripture, and some even questioned my faith. It was frightening to be challenged on the foundation of my recovery program, but God had brought me this far and I wasn't about to panic.

Don told me before I was discharged that he knew I was really improving when I was willing to disagree with someone, even if that meant having him or her angry with me. I hoped that my friends wouldn't get mad at me if we didn't see eye-to-eye on the issue of the whole "faith healing versus psychological help" issue. I was discovering that our differences were really ones of understanding, experience and Christian growth. I had come to realize in the past four months that no one is perfect except Jesus Christ; only He has all the answers. That knowledge made it easier to stay on track when my treatment decisions were questioned.

Avoidance and Denial

I noticed something about my friends, relatives and acquaintances immediately. It was an avoidance of feelings that they considered negative. Everyone was willing enough to express happiness and joy, but I didn't see much anger, sadness or grief. I recognized in them many of the ways that I used to deal with those emotions. Previously I expressed anger by using sarcasm or being passive-aggressive. For example I might say, "Well, I can understand that you must be very busy. It's not surprising that you don't have time to serve on a committee when your day is full of things like tennis league and ceramics classes." It was said with a smile on my face, but anger in my heart.

As for sadness, a friend of mine told me of a terrible situation in her marriage and then said, "Oh well, that's life," as though there was nothing to feel bad about. Before treatment, I would have agreed, avoiding the feelings that came with sad circumstances. Now my heart was tender, and I made a point of asking friends how they felt about things they shared with me. It was quite a change from the old me and it was wonderful to show them that I really cared.

We attended a great church. The staff loves and encourages the members to stay in God's Word and seek and follow His will for our lives. The church also has a strong outreach to the unsaved, both in our local area and through missions programs around the world. That's all good, godly and scriptural, but when I returned home I began to fume because I realized that for years I had gone to church, been involved in church activities and made many friends, yet I had no one with whom I could be open and honest. I sat in the pew with my family; makeup, hair and clothes perfect every Sunday. Everyone smiled at me and I smiled back, and all the time I was dying inside. Thinking that others would find me lacking spiritually if I admitted my problems and addiction, I was on a desert island amidst a sea of God's people.

Upon returning from treatment, I spoke to my pastor and his wife about my loneliness and fear of being the only Christian in the crowd with problems. They said that they never suspected that I had been alone and miserable. My mask was so skillfully constructed that it fooled them into thinking that I was fine, and my little family a model of happy godliness. That's when I began wondering if I had missed my calling. If I was that good an actress, I belonged on stage or in the movies!

My pastor also told me something amazing. There were many, many hurting people in our church. Some were better at hiding it than others, but I wasn't the only one in pain. They invited me to share a little of my story in a couples Sunday school classes that Scott and I attended.

Here was my first opportunity to be completely honest about myself. If I had the courage to let others see my worn spots, the "real" me, would they still love me? I had never been afraid to speak in public, but this time I was terrified. I knew in my heart that God wanted me to trust Him and be honest and share what He was doing in me.

Knees knocking, heart pounding and palms sweaty, I stood in front of about 50 people and began to tell them about my pain and loneliness, and about my family's frustration and confusion. I briefly sketched a verbal picture of my past, my eating disorder and what I learned in treatment. The saddest thing, I told them, was that there seemed to be no one in the Body of Christ I could turn to. That isolation only increased my shame because I felt I was the only Christian I knew who wasn't happy.

Scott sat at the front and held me with his gaze. I saw surprise on other faces, and compassion. After class, people offered hugs and words of encouragement. A sense of relief washed over me. I had talked about my feelings, told my secrets and it had turned out all right. It was a huge step in recovery.

Real at Last

A beautiful illustration of allowing others to see the real you is in the book, *The Velveteen Rabbit.* In the story, a stuffed rabbit and a toy horse are discussing why some toys considered themselves real and other toys were just, well, toys.

"What is REAL?" asked the Rabbit one day, when they were lying side by side near the nursery fender, before Nana came to tidy the room. "Does it mean having things that buzz inside you and a stick-out handle?"

"Real isn't how you are made," said the Skin Horse. "It's a thing that happens to you. When a child loves you for a long, long time, not just to play with, but REALLY loves you, then you become Real."

"Does it hurt?" asked the Rabbit?

"Sometimes," said the Skin Horse, for he was always truthful. "When you are Real you don't mind being hurt."

"Does it happen all at once, like being wound up," he asked, "or bit by bit?"

"It doesn't happen all at once," said the Skin Horse. "You become. It takes a long time. That's why it doesn't often happen to people who break easily, or have sharp edges, or who have to be carefully kept. Generally, by the time you are Real, most of your hair has been loved off, and your eyes drop out and you get loose in the joints and very shabby. But these things don't matter at all, because once you are Real you can't be ugly, except to people who don't understand." *

Finally, I was Real! I did feel very shabby, like parts of me had gotten worn off. I was emotionally tired and still tender in the places of my heart that were beginning to heal. The process of recovery was difficult and painful, but I came through it with people who loved me. God loved me even more, and He and my friends never gave up on me.

"I spent most of my life hoping that no one would see the real me, because if they did, they would certainly be grossed out. What a startling discovery and blessing to find that people loved me more when I was Real. It has continued to be true. Others are drawn to you and open themselves up when they realize there is no pretense in you. Of course a few can be hurtful, but like the Skin Horse said, when you are Real, you can't be ugly except to those who don't understand. True empathy comes when you have walked a hard road. Then you recognize and connect with others' pain.

My approach at work was very different. My coworkers in the National Guard were mostly men, and we were not close. I was friendly with a few of them, but I didn't feel comfortable sharing anything about my disorder or treatment with them. I told my boss the truth about my illness, and asked him to keep it confidential. I didn't think that sharing such personal information was appropriate in the workplace, and, quite honestly, I didn't trust the men I worked with to be kind if they found out. I told them that I had been ill and in the hospital, and left it at that. It felt good to make that decision and know that it was based on caring for myself rather than fear.

Eating disorders thrive in secrecy, and as I made healthy choices, I knew that truth would continue to set me free.

---

*Margery Williams, *The Velveteen Rabbit* (Crown Publishers, Inc. New York, New York, 1986), p. 13-14.

Living in Graceland

Grace strikes us when we are in great pain and restlessness... Sometimes at that moment a wave of light breaks into our darkness, and it is as though a voice were saying, "You are accepted."

—Paul Johannes Tillich, 1886-1965

Before I began my journey to wholeness, I didn't really know what forgiveness was. So many times in my life I had heard the term "forgive and forget." I believed that this was a biblical principle, that I should be able to forgive an offender and, in doing so, automatically forget the offense. That was the source of a lot of my guilt. There was nothing automatic about forgiveness or forgetting, and I assumed that if I couldn't, it was a shortcoming.

After months of therapy and teaching, I realized something. Feelings experienced because someone hurts you don't just immediately go away. Forgiveness is a process, and I was learning that the willingness and desire to forgive are just the first step. Somewhere I heard that the concept of forgiveness entails revisiting the offense and releasing the offender. That's a simple task if someone steps on your foot and asks for forgiveness right away, but I was dealing with offenses that were decades old. Revisiting the offense for me meant remembering what happened and acknowledging the feelings of hurt, anger, sadness and fear.

That had been the purpose of Process Group. Releasing the offender simply involved asking God to help me desire to forgive. Sometimes it helps to talk to the person who hurt you, but that's not always practical. I found that when the feelings were released, my anger began to melt. Over a period of years I have been able to forgive, and to actually feel the forgiveness in my heart.

Dealing with Guilt and Shame

Forgiveness wasn't the only area of my life where I struggled with guilt. For the most part, guilt was my constant companion.

Global guilt

If anything went wrong, I assumed it was my fault. My guilt was global and nonspecific. When my husband was angry about the erosion in the back yard, I felt guilty. Reading about starving children brought on guilt because I wasn't doing anything to help feed them. If the pastor asked for more Sunday school teachers from the pulpit, I felt selfish and remorseful for not anticipating the need and signing up to teach. Once, when we moved to a new city, I was driving my parents to a restaurant that I had only been to once. I got lost, and felt like a complete failure for not knowing the way and wasting their time when they were hungry. You name it—if it was wrong, uncomfortable or didn't fit in some way, it was my fault.

Information gleaned from treatment helped me see that guilt is often related to "shoulds" in one's childhood, and mine had plenty. "You should know better…you shouldn't have done that…I shouldn't have to tell you this…You shouldn't feel that way." Hygiene, behavior, grades and other achievements were motivated with "shoulds." I wanted to believe, and to have others believe, that I was smart enough to know things without being taught. If I *should* have known or done something and didn't, then I was either dumb or a slow learner. Anything I didn't do was laziness ("I *should* have…").

In turn, using guilt to motivate others came naturally for me because it worked to motivate me. Making others feel bad about themselves makes them want to change their behavior so that they can feel good, I reasoned; so I used "shoulds" and "oughts" with impunity on my husband, children and others.

My own guilt and anxiety level was always crippling. Nothing I did was good enough. A constant refrain running in my head said, "I should have known. I should have done it better."

There are two types of guilt. True guilt comes when we have done something to break the rules we live by. False guilt is assuming guilt for something you had no control over. Escape from true guilt includes accepting God's grace, and doing anything I can to make amends. Unkind words can be repaid with an apology and an act of kindness. Asking for forgiveness and offering to pay for the inconvenience is appropriate for missing an appointment or letting someone down.

When I feel guilty for something that is not my fault, I ask myself "What is the truth here? What could I have done to prevent this?" If the answer is "nothing," then it's false guilt, and worrying about it is a waste of time and energy. It takes practice, but it's easy once you get the hang of it.

Shame and the message, "I am bad"

Shame was my other constant companion. For most of my life, shame and guilt were indistinguishable for me. In both cases, I felt bad about myself. One of the most valuable lessons I learned in therapy was how to distinguish guilt from shame, then to decide if either emotion was really appropriate for me in the situation.

The new definitions made the two feelings clear. Shame says that I am bad or wrong. Guilt says that I *did* something bad or wrong. In both cases, there is an escape. God's grace covers both. In Romans 8:1, God assures us: "Therefore, there is now no condemnation for those who are in Christ Jesus."

With shame, I have to ask myself if I have done anything to deserve to feel that way. For me, true shame only serves one function and that is to bring me to repentance. If guilt says "I did something bad," and shame says, "I am bad," then first I must decide if I am indeed bad. If I have sinned and refuse to repent, then I deserve to feel ashamed. That is true shame, and the feeling serves to let me know I am out of God's will.

False shame comes when I not only take on responsibility for something that is not mine, but I also internalize the feelings and apply them to my value as a human being. God is ready and willing to cleanse me of my sin; He did it long ago when Jesus died for my sins. When I deserve to feel ashamed, righteousness is one sincere prayer away. False shame is denied with truth. If it's not my sin, then I can let go of the feelings of shame.

I could never fully be confident existing in the present, because I was always looking over my shoulder for some person or God to drop the hammer on me. I scrutinized my every thought, word and action, looking for blame. Putting everything under a magnifying glass led to indecision, fear and inaction, and eventually paralyzed me. The anxiety that dogged me for so long began to dissipate as I realized that mistakes are an inevitable outcome of trying new ideas and concepts. God's forgiveness is bigger than any mistake I could ever commit.

My therapist, Don, handed me a lifelong "Get out of guilt free" card when he told me that God is so powerful, He can use anything to serve His purposes. Even if I *really* mess something up, God can use it. To test the theory I asked, "What if I were to kill someone?"

Don's answer was typical for him. Intensely, but with humor, he replied, "I wouldn't recommend it as a good way to find out what God can do, but yes, He could use even that to serve His purpose." Then he said, "Sandy, you have been hurt. You are becoming a mended vessel as you heal, but remember this: A mended vessel is usually stronger than the original, and God can definitely use cracked pots."

"You Shall Know the Truth"

Truth was my new ally. Having learned the truth about my past I now knew that, while bad things had happened to me and I had made some bad choices, I am not a bad person. I was determined to live in truth. When old memories rose to haunt me, truth would keep me safe. If I stumbled in recovery, truth enabled me to keep going. Some of my most important recovery truths are:

- No one is perfect.
- Deviating from my dietary plan is not a disaster.
- I can ask people for help.
- Honesty about my feelings will help keep me well.
- My past does not define who I am today.

The whole truth is that as an imperfect person, I am allowed to make mistakes. Things are no longer so black and white.

Re-entering life at home, I was back in the same environment with the same stresses that had triggered eating disorder symptoms. I heard in my head the old lies that had fed my sickness and perfectionism. In their book *Telling Yourself the Truth*, William Backus and Ruth Chapin have listed the common that we believe. All of them were things that I told myself and consequently suffered. For instance, I really believed that:

- It is a terrible thing to have hurt feelings.
- If I do something, I must do it perfectly.
- I must avoid distress at all costs.
- I can't be happy unless everyone likes me.
- I have no choice about what happens to me.

Seeing through such lies helped me allow truth to become my cornerstone to healthy living. When guilt feelings arose, usually connected with a misbelief (or lie), instead of resorting to bingeing and purging, I sought the truth about the situation. I would literally take a break and ask myself the following questions:

- Who is responsible for this situation?
- If this task remains undone, will the sun still rise in the morning?
- What are my options in these circumstances?
- Will this moment in time be important in a few years?

Based on the answers to those questions, I would know how to respond to the feeling. Truth brought freedom from fear and guilt.

Feeling kind of alien

As I practiced what I learned in treatment, something amazing dawned on me. Not everyone wants to deal in the truth. Almost everyone I encountered denied feelings that made him or her uncomfortable. They actually spoke the old beliefs: "You have to…" or "You really should…" or "So and so made me feel…"

But I wanted to confront problems and feelings, talk about them honestly and work them out. After awhile I started to feel that I was a visitor from another planet. I came from the planet Recovery, and while I knew the language of the people on Earth, talking with them revealed that most do not speak openly and truthfully. Most hide behind masks of politeness and evasiveness.

Those of us who are overcoming addictions have to deal with truth, or we find ourselves back in our old destructive behaviors. Addicts are terrific at lying to themselves and others. Denial of the truth is what keeps us sick. People who either have had no compulsive behaviors or denied them seemed to believe the lies that had held me captive for so long. Now I knew that only the truth could set me free.

My link to the planet Recovery

Aftercare was my link to people like me, people who spoke my new language. Before I left treatment, the staff helped me contact professionals near my home who could reinforce and help me continue my new and healthier life. A therapist, a psychiatrist and a support group were among them. These people encouraged me and suggested ways to continue recovering in this "strange land."

I was seeing others and myself more clearly. Now aware of my motivations, I had a better idea of my strengths and weaknesses. Manipulation, blame shifting and shaming became choices rather than reactions. There was a new awareness that daily life was full of choices. How would I respond to people, circumstances and feelings? My goal was to act wisely, rather than to merely react.

New knowledge of myself enabled me to see others more clearly and to better understand their motivations. The challenge was to use the knowledge I had gained wisely. I had to learn to use my understanding of people to help me interact with them rather than trying to get them to change.

The Need for Balance

Like a new Christian, I was full of zeal for my new beliefs and way of life. Unfortunately, like many who are anxious to convert the unbeliever, I used my new truth indiscriminately. More than just living in truth, I had to learn when and how to use the truth.

A case of misguided zeal

I wanted everyone to experience the freedom and self-acceptance that I had found. I wanted so badly to share that I became an armchair psychologist, diagnosing others' pain and dispensing nuggets of counsel. Sometimes stating the truth was a defensive act, and not necessary or helpful.

Even now I still feel the pain of an incident that occurred four months out of treatment. I had a chance to spend two weeks with a dear friend whom I had not seen in a couple of years. She was a spiritual mentor to me, and a warm, fun friend. After a week with my children at her house, the normal irritations of living with another family began to surface. Our kids didn't always get along. Our stuff was all over her house. Cooking and cleaning for three extra people is stressful, even when the guests help. None of those things is the end of the world, but stress not talked about tends to seem worse than it really is.

One time in particular my friend became annoyed with Anne for spilling her milk. In frustration, she spoke sharply and Anne began to cry. As we did the dishes that night I said, "Is something bothering you? You seemed very upset about the spilled milk." She said that no, nothing was wrong. Then she slammed a cabinet door.

I tried again. "Is Anne getting on your nerves? Children can be irritating sometimes."

Again came the answer, "No," and this time it was punctuated with a pan banged into the sink.

I kept it up: "Well, you seem angry. I think you need to talk about it. Maybe you hold things inside until you explode with unjustified anger over a small incident."

Without looking at me she said, "I was raised to not get into matters like this. I believe that if you let it go, it will take care of itself."

"Oh no," I replied. "You have to talk about your feelings, otherwise you can't have healthy relationships. And it can affect your health, too," I added, pointedly looking at her generous figure.

She had once confided to me that she sometimes screamed at her husband in anger. I tried to use that as an illustration of what I was saying. "You know how you said that you yell at Jim? I'll bet if you two sat down and talked about all of the little things that are bothering you, it would keep you from getting so angry with him." Not surprisingly, the visit went downhill from that moment.

I am literally cringing as I write this. My intentions were good, but in my eagerness to help my friend with her anger management, I destroyed our friendship. There was no gradual exposure to the new and improved me. The last time we had been together, I was the queen of denial and a champion feeling-stuffer. Now, not only did I deal with things very differently, I had the gall to tell her that she had a problem.

What a disaster, and what a hard lesson. I have apologized several times, but I hurt her so badly with my clumsy attempt to "fix" her that she doesn't want to be my friend anymore. I can't change anyone with the truth, but I can hurt them with it if I'm not sensitive and careful.

Balancing self with others

Self-care is another area that requires balance. Balance usually comes after leaning too hard to one side or another until equilibrium is found. Prior to treatment, I believed that I must always be productive and put others before myself. In recovery I was serious about taking time for myself through therapy, reflection, journaling and relaxation. It was a change for me, and I struggled with guilt. It was a change for those around me, too.

Even the term "self-care" can raise eyebrows. It sounds selfish. What it actually means is that I make myself a priority along with everything and everyone else in my life. I had always believed that I had to sacrifice myself for others. Sacrifice has its place, but not to the point of resentment and exhaustion or guilt when I take time to enjoy something or simply to rest. Self-care is different for everyone, and those of us who are learning not to do too much usually have to be taught how to care for ourselves. I had to learn, for example, that to care for myself I need time to sit with my feet up and do nothing. I need an occasional nap. Exercise helps me stay healthy. Time alone is necessary so that I can think and reflect. It all feels selfish at first. So accustomed to always doing for others, it was difficult to adjust my priorities to include myself.

It's also difficult for the family of a compulsive "doer" when she begins to leave some things undone in order to devote necessary time to her own needs. Balance comes with time and practice. Since we're not perfect, we'll make mistakes when rearranging our priorities. That's why it is so important to realize that nothing is engraved in stone. Everything can be adjusted.

I see my life as a pendulum. When I'm learning to apply a new concept to myself, the pendulum swings pretty hard, and I end up banging the stops on both sides of the arc. First too little, then too much. Where self-care is concerned, I used to totally ignore my own needs and I was a very sick and tired person. While learning how to care for myself, sometimes I was a little too militant about it and neglected necessary tasks in order to focus on me. I went back and forth as I learned from experience. Gradually, the pendulum is swinging more gently as it reaches a workable middle ground. Balance is now the goal in all areas of my life—eating, relationships, work and play. After lots of trial and error and hard work, the pendulum doesn't swing as hard.

Stumbling Toward Balance

There were some wild swings before I reached this state of equilibrium. One of them occurred one night after an argument with Scott.

Anger and flirting with alcohol

I was so furious that I again had the urge to deal with my anger the way I used to. Too proud to allow myself that relapse, I decided that if I couldn't binge and purge, I would get drunk. Scott and I were on the way to eat at a restaurant, and I made him stop the car. I got out and walked the two miles back home, livid the whole way.

I tried all of the feelings-management techniques I knew, but I was still wild with anger. The two-mile walk hadn't had any effect, and now lying on the floor with the stereo headphones blasting Beethoven hadn't helped. Calling a friend and telling her about it only made her mad at Scott, too, and I didn't feel any better. I wanted so badly to binge and purge because I knew I'd get immediate relief. I didn't want to go back to that, but I wanted to be numb. That's when I had the brilliant idea to get drunk. After all, I hadn't been treated for alcoholism, so I told myself it wasn't like I'd be returning to my addiction.

I got in my car and drove to the liquor store. After parking behind the dumpster where I figured no one from church would see me, I went inside and bought a large bottle of beer. I went back to the car and drank it. I was still mad when it was gone. Back into the store, this time for wine coolers. After driving to the library and checking out a romance novel (to give me something else to think about), I drove to the lake and read my book and drank all of the wine coolers.

By then I was drunk and numb, and not nearly as angry as I had been. To ensure the feeling would last, I went back to the store and bought more beer and drank it. Obviously, truth wasn't having much of an effect on me at that moment. Too drunk to drive safely, but too ashamed to call for a ride, I drove home anyway. Collapsing on the couch in the basement, I called my therapist. I knew what I had done was stupid, but I wanted her to tell Scott about it so I wouldn't have to.

Wisely, she refused, and reminded me that I was responsible for my behavior—and its consequences. She also gently reminded me that I was allowed to make mistakes, and suggested I say something to Scott along the lines of "I goofed, Dear. Can we talk about it in the morning?" Scott wasn't very happy with me, and the hangover I had the next day convinced me not to use alcohol to deal with feelings again.

Fear and a bulimic relapse

I also had one bulimic relapse that lasted about a week before I realized that I didn't want to live with my head in the toilet anymore.

I was on a trip with the Air National Guard and, over the phone, Scott and I had a discussion that became heated. I felt terribly impotent because I wanted to deal with the situation and resolve it right then, but there was no way to do that. We weren't getting very far on the phone, and I wasn't due to go home for another week. Again, my feelings overwhelmed me. This time it was fear. I convinced myself that my marriage was over, based on the things we had said in anger over the phone.

I was in charge of six jets and the people who maintained them, and we had a schedule of flying and maintenance to keep. Afraid that I couldn't do my job in such an emotional state, I also realized that drinking to relieve the pain wasn't a useful option. I toyed with the idea of not eating, rationalizing that it would numb my feelings, and I wouldn't be guilty of going back to bingeing and purging. The more I thought about it, the better it sounded. It would not only help me feel better, when I went home thinner, Scott would be really sorry that he had said those things.

I began by fasting and drinking only juice, but the men who worked for me asked me why I wasn't eating with them. So I ate small amounts with them in the mess hall and then vomited it all back up later. I told them that I had the stomach flu, and quit eating again. By the time I got home, I had lost several pounds and was severely dehydrated. Scott met me at the airport with a smile and a hug and apologized for getting mad at me on the phone. As far as he was concerned, we had had a spat, and it was really no big deal. He was right. I blew it all out of proportion in my mind, and allowed my emotions to get out of control.

Relapsing into my old behavior was scary, but this time it was different. I knew exactly what I was doing, and why. Choosing to deal with a problem in an unhealthy manner was very different from being caught up in an addiction I didn't understand. Putting the incident behind me, I began eating again. I decided that I never wanted to live with my head in the toilet again, and that I wasn't going to starve to get anyone's attention.

Using the knowledge I had gained in treatment and with the help of the therapist I was seeing in aftercare, I learned something very useful from my relapse. My fear of being abandoned by Scott was directly related to my feelings about losing my father. Fighting with my stepfather during my teens had reinforced my feelings that someone who was angry with me couldn't love me. Putting all of this information together, I reminded myself that Scott was neither one of my fathers. He was my husband, and he could indeed love me and be mad at me at the same time. He said that he would never desert me, and it was up to me to believe that, or wallow in insecurity every time we had a quarrel or misunderstanding. That is only one example of how the insight I gained through therapy has helped me live a much happier and more emotionally stable life.

New Tools Along the Way

Nine months out of treatment, I was well on my way to recovery. It wasn't easy, but my obsession with food and weight was diminishing. My relationships were much more stable, and I was learning more about myself every day. Like a butterfly emerging from its cocoon, I was a very different creature from what I had been four months earlier. Also like a butterfly, my wings were wet and fragile as I entered a new phase of my life. I was changed, but everyone else was the same. The stresses that triggered eating disorder symptoms were still there.

Luckily, treatment hadn't just broken the addictive component of my disease and then sent me home. I was well equipped with a tool belt full of healthy ways to cope. At its simplest, an eating disorder is a coping mechanism—crude and dangerous to be sure, but it effectively dulls feelings and gives a temporary and false sense of well-being.

My new tools would not dull pain or remove stress, but they would help me cope with them. Things like a local therapist, a support group, friends whom I could call any time and a dietary plan to use at home were a few of those tools. I had a notebook full of insights I had learned in treatment. I could journal my feelings, tell myself the truth about the situation or realize that feelings are temporary and just sit tight until the emotion began to pass and I could see the situation more rationally.

Family Factors

The "honeymoon" period of being home was over in a few weeks, and I got down to the nuts and bolts of living my same old life in a whole new way. This time, I tried to make my husband and my girls a priority.

Revising my parenting

Anne and Lauren were too young to understand eating disorders, but I had told them that I was sick. The tricky part was getting a four-year-old and a six-year-old to understand that I was still getting well when I had never really looked sick in their young eyes.

One of the first different things that Anne noticed about me was the food that I served the family and ate myself. For the first time she could remember, red meat showed up regularly on our table. Food fascist that I was, I had told my children and Scott that red meat wasn't fit for human consumption. "Heart attack on a plate" is what I actually called it. Scott just went along with me at home, and ate burgers and steaks when he was on the road. The girls simply ate what I fixed for them. Now I had to tell them that part of my sickness was thinking that certain foods are "bad" and must be avoided. Anne, who is one smart kid and hadn't tasted refined sugar until she was two, caught on fast. She started asking me for foods she had seen only in commercials or at friends' houses, like hot dogs and cereal with marshmallow surprises!

While I had eaten a variety of what I considered "forbidden" foods in treatment, grocery shopping at home was where the rubber met the road. It was scary at first, but became fun. The girls were awestruck the first time I offered them a donut after they had eaten their oatmeal. Their eyes were huge, and they grinned as they got powdered sugar all over their faces.

The area of parenting that I felt the most urgency to change was using shame to motivate my children. Seeing the crushing effect of shame in my own life was my motivation to learn new parenting techniques. I had used shame to control the girls' behavior because it worked, and I didn't understand how damaging it was. Instead of saying "You should be ashamed of yourself for treating your sister that way," a healthier alternative was "I know she frustrates you, but hitting isn't OK. Let's find a different way to deal with the problem."

When I was bingeing, purging and starving, it was very easy to tune my kids out. My interaction with them was pretty much limited to caring for their physical needs and making them look perfect so that I would look good to others. I loved them, but having built so many walls around my heart, I couldn't be totally available to them emotionally. Now I could really connect with them, understand them and be a better mom. Not that it's easy. Many of my outpatient therapy sessions have centered on the frustrations of motherhood. Now that the girls are teenagers, we have a whole different set of challenges. The good news is that I'm emotionally here for them, and we trust each other. Occasionally wanting to wring each other's neck is just part of the total picture. What gives us hope is that we're talking about the issue and loving each other.

Husband-wife relationships

As I shed my cocoon and tested my new wings, I felt the most vulnerable in my relationship with Scott. We literally laid the foundation for a better marriage when he visited me in treatment during Family Week. We had a long way to go, and we weren't sure what our marriage would look like when we were done, but we wanted to be closer, understand and trust each other more and get along better.

The most immediate and obvious area to discuss and work on was also the most intimate. We were apart for almost four months. We both wanted to restart our sexual relationship, but something stood in the way. Scott had not known about the sexual abuse in my past until Family Week. Knowing how injured I was in that area answered many questions, but also left him unsure about how to approach me.

As for me, I was eager to be intimate yet disturbed by the memories that were now fresh in my mind. I was thinking, "Does he still want me now that he knows what I've experienced?" and "What if we get started and I freak out?" Scott wondered, "Does she still want me after all that she's remembered?" and "What if we get going and she freaks out?"

As with everything, honesty is the key. We talked about it, tentatively at first, then with more confidence, knowing that we had similar misgivings. We agreed that if I felt uncomfortable or frightened I would tell him and we would stop. It was awkward at first, but it got easier. For me, being released from the shame in my past gave me freedom in an area that I thought would always be difficult.

Scott and I discovered many things to work through as I reintegrated into the family. He had run the house and raised the kids while I was gone, and he didn't do things the way I did them. My old compulsions resurfaced as I found that things were moved and routines changed. I wanted it my way. The girls now put their own laundry away, the refrigerator was in disarray and my Tupperware lids were no longer in order by size. I heard a lot of "Daddy doesn't do it that way." For a while it was hard to remember that safety doesn't come from having all of my ducks in a row. We had many power struggles as the balance of responsibilities shifted.

Steps Toward Staying Healthy

Without a support system waiting for me when I got home, I wouldn't have maintained "sobriety," refraining from bingeing and purging. There were so many times when I felt overwhelmed and afraid. I knew how effectively my eating disorder dulled feelings, and was frequently tempted.

During treatment I did some research and made phone calls so I could have an appointment for therapy waiting for me when I got home. I hadn't met the therapist, although he came highly recommended. However, after several visits to his office it was clear to me that we weren't connecting. He wanted to cover ground that I had recently traveled.

After trying two other therapists, I found one who really understood eating disorder issues and was willing to design a treatment program that picked up my therapy where it had left off at the Ranch. Meeting weekly at first, we gradually tapered off to once a month. We discussed my food and relationship fears, parenting concerns and self-image. After two years, I had the confidence to go it alone, only calling for an appointment if I got "stuck" and couldn't put an issue in perspective.

Feeling less fragile as time went by, I was developing the self-confidence to assess each situation as it arose. Using techniques and information learned through reading and therapy, pinpointing how I felt and why I felt that way became more natural. My analogy is that problems used to hit me before I even saw them coming. Then, for a while, I'd see something approaching, but couldn't get out of the way in time, so I still got smacked. Finally, I would see a problem coming, process it and either neatly catch it or sidestep it altogether.

Staying healthy is my goal. To do this I have to be able to sort out and deal with issues. The key is the ability to connect my past to my present. Without that, I still get caught up in feelings that may have applied to something that happened long ago, but aren't appropriate for what is happening in the present. Old habits die hard, but now I have plenty of opportunities to see others and myself in the light of God's grace.

Along the Road

Sometimes I go back down to the basement of my soul. It's not as scary now, but it's still not a place I really like to visit. There's no lock on the door, and nothing bad is hiding there. The memories lost their power when I faced them. The brown ooze is gone—it was mopped up and disposed of with the last of my shame. Shadows of the memories of my past will never be gone, but they can't hurt me any more.

Dealing with the Past

When pain returns with a memory, I find that forgiveness is a task I must go back and do again. Now and then my past actions and the things done to me still color the way I feel about myself. At times I become angry with those who hurt me, but now I can combat those feelings with the truth. I have chosen to forgive others, and God has forgiven me. I know that I am not bad, in spite of poor choices I have made.

While I'm not bitter about the things that have happened in my life, I do have some regrets. Because I was too wrapped up in my misery to experience life, I feel cheated of some of the pleasures of growing up. I envy friends who fondly reminisce about high school and college. A crushing lack of confidence kept me from making friends and having fun.

An invitation to a high school reunion used to terrify me because I still felt like an outsider. Now I just feel sad that I feel no affection for anyone from that time in my life. Even today when I get a newsletter from the university I attended, I throw it away unread. There is no kinship, no sense of belonging. I go to Scott's reunions with him, and wish I could experience the lifelong comradeship he has with his high school and college buddies.

Measures of Recovery

People often ask me how long it takes to get over an eating disorder. I don't think there is one answer to fit each individual in recovery. In my case, after about two years my obsession with food was gone. I no longer felt the desire to binge, purge or starve. I eat to live, rather than living to eat.

Another significant measure of my recovery is how I see my body. Gaining a few pounds doesn't inspire panic. I don't want to become obese, but I have a more realistic definition of "overweight." My litmus test for being overweight used to be that my thighs must not touch when I walked or stood with my legs together. Now, my thighs enjoy a close relationship and it doesn't bother me.

That doesn't mean I don't have my "fat" days. When I'm feeling insecure about an important issue, my focus usually goes to my stomach and hips. Examples of things that I'm sometimes vulnerable about are my job, my ability to parent and how good a wife I am. My tendency when I'm unsure is still to grab for something I can control—like my weight. When I find that I'm holding my stomach in and obsessing about every bite I eat, I know it's time to concentrate on the real source of my self-doubt. Episodes of feeling fat never last long, now that I can focus on the real problem. As with most things in recovery, it takes practice, but it gets easier.

I can say that I am recovered because I'm satisfied with the size and shape of my body. I attack problems, rather than running from them, or assaulting myself. When I start to imagine that losing 10 pounds will improve my life, I think back to when I was thinnest. When I weighed 104, I was frequently ill and living in a prison of fear. Remembering the days when I measured my worth by whether or not size five jeans fit is always enough to get me back into a healthy mind-set where I can identify and work on what is really bothering me.

There is freedom in eating without obsessing. I eat what I like, and try to stay within a healthy weight range. Food is a delight, now that I am no longer its slave. Sometimes I overeat, but I no longer starve myself or purge to compensate. The key to determining why I have overeaten lies in asking why I ate so much. Usually it's because it tastes good or I ate too fast. Portion control and enjoying each bite solves that. I still overeat for emotional reasons now and then. Boredom, anxiety and anger can all find me in the kitchen nibbling. Again, asking "Why?" helps. Once I've pinpointed the emotion and I realize that no amount of M & Ms or cookies will help, the desire to overeat is gone.

Cultural Roots of Eating Disorders

While my past is the root of my eating disorder, other factors contributed to it. I believe that society's preoccupation with physical beauty, specifically thinness, is partly what prompted my hatred of my body. Eating disorders not only have symptoms such as purging and starving, but also false beliefs and distorted thinking. Recovery is comprised of stopping the destructive behaviors, restructuring thoughts and changing beliefs.

Even women who don't have an eating disorder tend to equate self-esteem with dress size. We live in a society that values thinness in women above nearly every other attribute. Beautiful is defined as thin, and we are confronted with this ideal everywhere we turn. Advertising, movies, TV, magazines, sports, music videos and practically every other medium bombard us with pictures of how women are "supposed" to look. It is burned into our psyche at a very young age that thin means pretty, energetic and healthy.

On the other hand, we are led to believe that "fat" means ugly, lazy and unhealthy. What a lie. In the first place, society's definition of "fat" is wrong. In the second place, God created each of us as an individual, and He did not give fewer brains, less talent, personality or good looks to those who are more amply endowed.

As early as elementary school, girls become convinced that their self-worth is based upon their appearance. When a young girl's body is preparing for puberty, she begins to put on weight. Fat is a precursor for hormone production, and her body prepares itself accordingly. Unfortunately, young girls are conditioned to believe that fat is bad, and they misinterpret the change in their bodies as unhealthy weight gain. Desire to diet is a common reaction. Equally unfortunate is the fact that many of these girls' mothers are preoccupied with their own weight, and the girl is conditioned to diet as she observes her mother's behavior.

Dieting is sadly common in girls as young as nine or 10. It has been shown that girls who start dieting before age 14 are eight times more likely to develop an eating disorder. The unrealistic image of perfection that society holds up to us breeds dissatisfaction with ourselves even as children.

Recovering from an eating disorder requires a radical change of mind. The professionals who are helping us get well teach us that appearance isn't the most important thing. That knowledge becomes a lifeline as we put our lives back together. At the same time, we still have to live in a thin-obsessed, beauty-worshipping culture.

The only way I can survive is to have "an attitude." Deliberately I mentally refute the notion that I must be thin and perfect to be beautiful or worthwhile. It's become my soapbox, and my girls can mouth the words along with me as I lecture on the danger of equating personal value with a number on a scale. My attitude is what keeps me from comparing myself to the waifs strutting the latest fashion down a Paris runway. I can go to the public pool and not hide under a towel because I truly believe that my mental and physical health is more important than looking like an adolescent boy in a bathing suit.

Approximately 30 percent of high school and college girls have eating disorders, and 1 percent of teenage girls and 5 percent of college girls become anorexic or bulimic. It happens because unique individuals feel that they have to cram themselves into the same thin mold.

As I mentioned before, adult women are also caught up in a dieting mind-set. All of us tend to think that we are above average in weight, but the truth is that the average woman in our society is 5'4" and weighs 142 pounds. The average model is 5'10" and weighs 112 pounds. Why do we accept representation by women who are nowhere near normal?

Society and the media might be culprits in promoting unrealistic images of beauty, but responsibility for our own well-being lies with us. We must manage our feelings and have practical physical expectations of our bodies to stay healthy.

The Joy of Staying Untangled

Have you ever reached into your jewelry box for a necklace and pulled out a snarl of delicate chains? If you pull at them too hard to untangle them, one will probably break. You can either very patiently work at them until they separate, or decide not to wear a necklace.

That's what I was like emotionally before I decided to get treatment for my eating disorder. The tangle of emotions inside me was too overwhelming to face, so I distracted myself with food. I've learned to store my necklaces separately so they won't become a mess. Similarly, I deal with my feelings one at a time now instead of carelessly shoving them all together. Treatment helped me gently untangle my emotions, and a large part of recovery is keeping up with them so they don't get out of control again.

Tuning in and teaching

Recovery, and staying "untangled," gives me the ability to be in tune with people on a very different level. I listen to what they are saying—as well as to what they're not saying. I can identify with others' pain because I have experienced pain of my own.

As I grew more confident in my recovery, I began to share my dysfunctional past and details about my eating disorder. The people I talked to at my church passed my story on to others, and wounded Christians began to come out of the woodwork. Not all of them struggled with an eating disorder, but they had problems or addictions that severely affected their lives. They were drawn to me like a magnet, not just because I admitted that I wasn't perfect, but also because I talked about help and hope. They asked me how I had come to a place of peace and healing. I realized that most of the principles such as honesty and vulnerability I had learned during recovery apply to most situations in which people are in emotional pain.

Looking back over my therapy and teaching notes from treatment, I saw an opportunity to lead an adult Sunday school class. Many years ago, my pastor's wife asked me to teach adults. I was already teaching children, and I truly believed I had nothing to offer to adults. Now, as I built a syllabus for the class, I was both excited and nervous. I really wanted to share what God had been teaching me, but I was afraid that either no one would show up or that the class would bomb.

I arrived early the first Sunday, and went to my assigned room—where I found half of the 40 seats already filled. After walking out into the hall to check the number on the door and making sure I was in the right room, I watched in amazement as the chairs continued to fill. By the time class started, we needed a few more chairs. The class was called "Hurts and Healing," and looking at all of those faces told me just how many wounded Christians were in my church.

The class was a success, not because of me but because the time was right for God to begin working in these people's hearts. Honestly, I don't know why God chose me to begin the process of recognizing that there are many wounded soldiers in His army. I'm humbled that He trusted me, though. Pastors on the church staff made themselves available to counsel those who needed it, and the church sponsored support groups. People with eating disorders, alcoholism and other addictions found acceptance, fellowship and hope that they could overcome their problems.

I have taught about emotional healing and self-esteem several times. Some of my very best friends were strangers who showed up in my classes to work on personal growth and became very dear to me. I love it when people trust me enough to share their hearts. It makes all of my pain worthwhile when I can encourage others. It is a measure of how much I have healed that I can share my past. And I consider it an honor when someone allows me into her soul's secret place.

Companionship—divine and human

Many people don't need, understand or desire recovery. It's a lonely business when you feel you're the only one who really wants to live in truth and work on personal growth. But once you begin your journey to wholeness, you never have to walk alone. God is with you every step of the way, and He will provide human companionship for you as well.

Ask God for someone to encourage, and you'll find He will answer your prayer by providing someone who can encourage you in return. Support groups are a great place to find other people who are tired of denial and want to work on recovery.

It would be great if we could completely forget old hurts. I'd like to live my days unencumbered by the past. However, my emotional wounds reach out and touch many areas of my life. For instance, there is still a hunger for love in my soul. A tender and vulnerable place in me remembers exactly what it felt like to be a hurting little girl who wanted her daddy. I get irritated when the little girl part of me takes over and I am lonely even amid those who truly care for me. Remembering that God is the only one who can satisfy the longings of my heart allows me to reassure little Sandy. Then I can more easily appreciate the caring that others offer me.

Leftovers Again?

Once in awhile I wonder if things that happened so long ago will haunt me forever. I think the answer is that I will sometimes struggle with feelings left over from old wounds. That probably explains my reluctance to pay a visit to my inner basement. The ghosts of images that remain remind me I have emotional areas that feel unprotected. The good news is that I now know how to deal with those sensitive places and the hunger in my soul. I combat lies with truth and fear with concrete examples that I am not alone.

Doses of reality

Staying healthy means dealing with reality rather than running from it. Unfortunately, reality isn't always pretty; in fact, at times it's just plain ugly. Some days are a challenge from start to finish. Life constantly throws curve balls that seem to come out of the blue. Traffic tickets, death of loved ones, disagreements and arguments with Scott and the challenges of motherhood catch me unaware many times.

Sometimes uncomfortable feelings still follow a negative experience. Absolute horror and remorse hit me after I illegally passed a school bus because I wasn't paying attention. It didn't help when the next morning, as we were eating breakfast, a sheriff's deputy came to the door and asked to speak to me. In my pajamas and robe and feeling extremely sheepish, I listened as he explained that the bus driver had taken my car's license plate number and reported me. Then he presented me with a $300 traffic citation for my little lapse.

Not long after that incident, I was doing my 20 minutes on the treadmill when the doorbell rang. The lady on my porch asked if those horses running down the street belonged to me. Sure enough, someone had left a gate open. As I chased them through the snow (wearing a tank top, shorts and boots), I wanted to seriously hurt whoever was responsible. Once the horses were safely home and the adrenaline from fear and anger was gone, the doorbell rang again. It was my buddy, the sheriff's deputy, responding to a report of horses on the road. No ticket this time, just a lecture and a warning.

At that moment, all I wanted to do was find out who left the gate open and give them a lecture. Even after years of therapy, I still sometimes think that placing blame is the first step to problem solving. A few minutes (or hours) of reflection usually calms me and I remember that blaming doesn't solve the problem.

Later that year, I got a speeding ticket, on my 40th birthday, no less. That unpleasant reality check cost $180. And it was topped off by one of my teenagers suggesting that I ask for a "frequent offender's" card with the sheriff's department. "Just think, Mom," she said, "all of the deputies know you by name now, and after 12 offenses, you can get free court costs!" I can laugh at it now, but it wasn't funny at the time. There was nowhere to run and nowhere to hide from the fact that life isn't always easy or fair.

Living with limitations

Losing my temper and screaming at my children leaves me wondering if they'll need therapy because of me. In reality, those episodes provide me with an opportunity to admit to them that I'm very human. I can apologize, then deal with their behavior in a much more reasonable manner.

I am embarrassed and furious with myself when I have completely forgotten an important commitment and let someone down. It happens frequently because, unfortunately, a good memory isn't my strongest suit. Rather than believe that I'm hopeless, I've become very good at making amends, and much more responsible about writing things down. Now I tend to put my appointments down for the wrong day and have to keep reminding others and myself that I'm not perfect.

I expected recovery to protect me from pain, but it doesn't. I believed that if I did everything right, life wouldn't hurt anymore, but it does. Before therapy, when distressing situations arose in spite of my efforts, I would become depressed as I struggled to "make everything turn out all right." It bothered me when a situation was unresolved and someone had hurt feelings or was unhappy. Through a long and painful process of trying to orchestrate happy endings and failing, God has shown me that trying to create happy endings is futile. I can't control the responses of others, and sometimes nothing I could do would fix the problem.

A current illustration concerns my health. I was diagnosed with fibromyalgia a few years ago. It's a central nervous system disorder, and the main symptoms are muscle pain and fatigue. These symptoms don't bother me every day, but they are an irritant. Sometimes they flare up enough to slow me down and occasionally knock me flat. The only recourse is to increase my self-care by getting more rest. I get frustrated when that happens, but since I know that the problem isn't degenerative, I don't worry. Instead, exercise, stress management, enough sleep and prayer lessen the severity and duration of the symptoms.

The biggest problem that I have with this condition concerns Scott's reaction to it. He has walked with me through my eating disorder and emotional problems, and wants me healthy. Our life together is relatively smooth this far into my recovery, but he always wonders what, if anything, will happen next. When he can see that I'm in pain or worn out, he gets upset. At a time when I could use a few kind words or a backrub, he wants less contact with me. He's not mad at me when he withdraws, but I interpret his lack of empathy as anger. I feel abandoned.

Scott's approval is still important to me, and the old fear of being unloved surfaces. I berate myself for feeling bad, and him for being insensitive. There is no known "cure" for fibromyalgia. Sometimes it goes away, and sometimes it doesn't. It's a small part of my life, but touches on my insecurity and need to feel loved and accepted by my husband. I can't change my condition, and I hate that. All I can do is trust God that Scott and I will grow through these situations. I can't change Scott's reaction to my illness, but I can control my responses to him.

I want peace in my marriage. Unfortunately, I can't control or change circumstances, and fighting them only leads to frustration and depression. Help and hope come when I take responsibility for my actions, forgive those who have hurt me, seek forgiveness from those I have hurt and trust God with the rest. When my heart's motives are in line with God's Word, He gives me the strength and grace I need in any predicament.

My objective as I move toward wellness is to deal with reality every day, identify and acknowledge my feelings and be open to the areas where God wants me to grow. When I feel overwhelmed, that's my cue to turn the problem over to God and let Him control the outcome.

I have a microwave mentality—when something is bothering me, I want it dealt with right away. My biggest challenge is to give a situation to God and then not snatch it back when it's not resolved immediately. He is showing me that I won't always like the outcome, but I still have to trust Him. To me, that's the essence of faith. God always lets me know what my part is in resolving a problem, then I'm supposed to get out of the way and let Him find the solution. I have to trust that His plan is always good, even when I don't understand it.

Opportunities, not mistakes

The most valuable discovery I have made along the road is that there are no mistakes in recovery. Poor choices? Yes. Overwhelming day? Definitely. Times when I don't care? Yes. Discouragement? Absolutely. Situations that I don't handle very well? Frequently. But these aren't mistakes. They're opportunities to learn—and grow.

"Mistake" sounds so final. "Opportunity" leaves the door open to do things differently the next time, or even to go back in that instance and try it another way. There's no rule about how many times you can say "I'm sorry," or try again. You've got the rest of your life to figure it out. Ask for help. Call a friend or your therapist. Seek God's wisdom. *Don't give up.*

Say it with me: *There are no mistakes in recovery, only opportunities to learn and grow.* Write it down. Tape it to your mirror. Carry it with you. Ease up on yourself.

I love my pilgrimage toward health and growth because I have learned to find delight in life as I walk along the road. Nothing in my path can separate me from the love of God. Romans 8:38 says: "For I am convinced that neither death nor life, neither angels nor demons, neither the present nor the future, nor any powers, neither height nor depth, nor anything else in all creation will be able to separate us from the love of God that is in Christ Jesus our Lord."

There is indescribable joy in my journey, regardless of circumstances or how I feel. Peace comes with the realization that no matter what is waiting around the next bend, God will give me the grace to overcome.

Soul Hunger
Order Form

Postal orders: The Remuda Cornerstone Bookstore
48 N. Tegner Street
Wickenburg, AZ 85390

Telephone orders: 1-800-445-1900 ext.4242

E-mail orders: cornerstone@remudaranch.com

Please send *Soul Hunger* to:

Name: ______________________________

Address: ______________________________

City: ____________________ State: __________

Zip: ____________ Telephone: (_____) ____________

Book Price: $14.99

Shipping: $3.00 for the first book and $1.00 for each additional book to cover shipping and handling within US, Canada, and Mexico. International orders add $6.00 for the first book and $2.00 for each additional book.

Or order from:
ACW Press
P.O. Box 110390
Nashville, TN 37222

(800) 931-BOOK

or contact your local bookstore